SITUATED

OBJECTS

Situated Objects

Buildings and Projects by Stan Allen
Photographs by Scott Benedict

PARK BOOKS

"Things that exist exist,
and everything is on their side."

Donald Judd

Situated Objects

Christian Herron (Delay Tactics), *Homage to Lewis Baltz*

BUILDING AND DRAWING

Architecture operates under a complex but rarely acknowledged paradox. Buildings, landscapes, and cities are durable physical entities, situated in the world and bound to place. Yet the working tools of the architect are ephemeral and highly abstract: drawings, diagrams, computer models, and mathematical calculations. As Robin Evans succinctly put it, "Architects don't make buildings, they make drawings for buildings." Architects work in the studio, at a distance from the building site, and they communicate their intentions through a series of codified notations. In large part, the intricacies of architectural practice revolve around navigating this divide, now made more complicated by digital technologies and the global nature of practice today.

A similar split polarizes the discipline as well. An architecture that begins and ends with building defines light, material, and space as architecture's essential characteristics. Any compromise

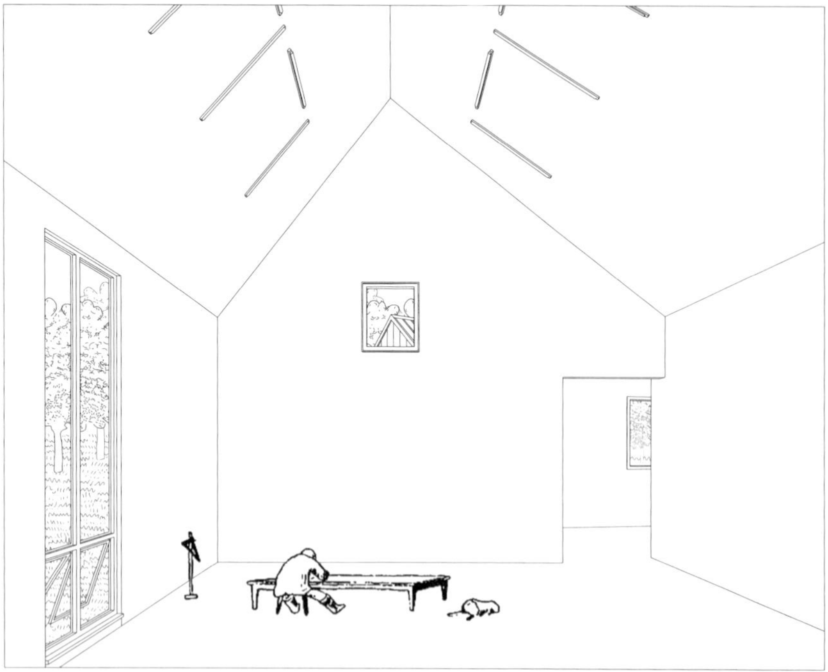

Stan Allen Architect,
E/S Studio, Milan, NY, 2019;
perspective

with abstract notation divorces the work from the hard logic of tectonics, risking a shallow and inauthentic architecture. For some architects and critics, however, this defines architecture too narrowly. They argue that it is precisely architecture's more abstract, representational character that allows it to take its place in the world of ideas, as a cultural practice among other cultural practices. The ability of the building to produce meaning, and to work within the logic of a representational system, is placed above the obstinate constructed reality of the building itself. They understand architecture as one aspect of an image-driven culture that includes books, exhibitions, competition projects, writing, and teaching: a broad array of discursive practices that may or may not have their definitive expression in the form of buildings.

Like many polarizing debates, this one has proven unproductive. Is there such a bright line between tectonics and representation? Making architecture involves both drawing *and* building. Issues of representation are deeply imbedded in the history of the discipline, and architecture's engagement with drawing is technical and instrumental as much as it is cultural. Drawing allows the architect to operate effectively between the abstract and the real. An argument for building does not have to be an argument for essentialist values of light, space, and experience. Beyond its raw physicality, a building is also a cipher in a social system, an artifact that produces meaning in an unscripted encounter with citizens who bring to it their own experiences, associations, and memories. Moreover, the process of building is complex and involves many agents. The architect has no other choice but to employ complex artifice in order to construct something new; but architecture needs to do more than simply register the story of its making. It needs to be robust enough to take its place in the world, independent of the support of its multiple authors.

Adolf Loos' essay "Architecture" (1910) begins with a description of a mountain lake: "The sky is blue, the water green and everywhere is profound tranquility." But that peace is disturbed by an "unnecessary screech." A villa, built by an architect. Why is it, Loos asks, that "every architect, good or bad, violates the lake?" Loos (who famously distrusted drawing) contrasts the work of the educated, city-dwelling architect with the artisan builder who works with local materials and shared know-how: "He is making a roof. What kind of roof? One that is beautiful or ugly? He does not know. The roof."

Loos tells a simple story that evokes the memory of an architecture that speaks to the collective imagination—"the visible expression of a point of view that others wish to share," as Mies van der Rohe would put it several decades later. We are far too self-conscious today to return to Loos' unreflective artisan builder, and the world has changed in ways that Loos could never imagine. Modernity was, in large part, the undoing of that unreflective relationship to a shared local knowledge. And yet, if architecture is going to continue to matter, architects need to get beyond questions of personal expression and the unrelenting search for novelty. They need to find ways to make visible that larger, shared understanding that gives architecture its social purchase. At a time when reproduced images and mass media dominate the cultural landscape, architecture's ability to work directly on the real is perhaps more urgent than ever. Buildings can and should function effectively in this double register: as designed artifacts, the product of disciplinary argument and matters of concern, and as factual objects in the world. The architect works simultaneously on the horizon of imagination—expanding the limit of the possible—and with an obstinate and inconsistent reality.

Stan Allen Architect, Sagaponac House, Sagaponac, Long Island, 2008.
Photo: Michal Moran

The drawings, writings, and photographs collected here document seven years of an architect's work: houses, studios, and temporary constructions. The buildings and projects in the book occupy the space between tectonics and representation. They encompass both architecture as a cultural practice and the reality of built work on site—what James Agee once called "the cruel radiance of what is." The book sets out to describe both the rich and untranslatable experience of architecture in its fully realized material form as well as the architect's working process. Photography, which belongs at once to the culture of images and to factual reality, offers a privileged point of entry. Photographs accept the constructed nature of

Stan Allen Architect, M/M House & Studio, Cold Spring, NY, 2013. Photo: Michael Biondo

the image as a starting point, but are also uniquely capable of presenting a series of approximations that approach the reality of the building and the complexity of its place in the landscape. In fact, what will never be present in the book is the architecture *per se*. Buildings deserve to live in time, to be inhabited and encountered in the world. Only in this way can they become part of the everyday lives of citizens and take their place in a shared social landscape.

Most of these projects are located in New York's Hudson River Valley, and all are on the East Coast of the United States, on rural or semi-rural sites. They are the product of a particular way of working, expressed in an attitude towards site, materials, building techniques, formal language, and design strategies. They form part of the landscape where I live and work, which has allowed me to follow the process of construction closely. Together, they reflect on the relationship between architecture and landscape at a time when human impact on the climate may have reached a tipping point.

The first task in any building project is to prepare the site. Construction may be a positive act, but it begins with destruction. In a town or a city, existing structures have to be demolished; on a rural site, trees have to be cut down, and earth has to be moved. Raw materials and heavy equipment need to arrive on the site. These are all brutal and messy operations. At a larger scale, the creation of building materials involves a systematic destruction of resources: harvesting timber, extracting minerals, and manufacturing metals, glass, and plastics. Even a small interior renovation requires the removal of existing partitions. The demolition plan is often the first drawing in a set of construction drawings: it is a blueprint for destruction.

Clearing and leveling a plot of ground is one of architecture's most elemental acts. In traditional cultures there are complex rituals around clearing the forest, breaking ground for foundations, or establishing a village. It is a rite of passage in which the land itself is passing from one state to another. Architecture's unique characteristic, distinct from the other plastic arts, is its relationship to place. Buildings are "situated" objects: object-like, in that they have fixed limits and stand free; situated, in that buildings always exist in an intricate relationship with a larger context. Landscape, pathways, views, the geology of the site, local ecologies, and local histories all figure into—and are figured by—the building. Architects often speak of a dialogue with the site, but that is not quite right. The act of building transforms the ground: cutting, scraping away, and reforming it to accommodate an unnatural presence. The architect does not so much fit the building to the land as fit the land to the building.

But if architecture is fixed in place, it also persists over time. The ground repairs itself, materials weather with age, rituals of use and habitation change with time. Site and building co-evolve to form a new whole. Houses and buildings structure the lives that take place within them in a complex interplay with a larger sense of place. Scale matters: buildings are bigger than we are. They provide shelter and symbolically mark the landscape. At the same time, a building does not end at its walls; it is a nexus in a complex field of social relations, cultural norms, and local histories. If building means remaking the landscape, the building also makes the landscape visible: landscape is architecture's inevitable foreground and counterpoint. Architecture and landscape collaborate to create a sense of place, and construct history over time.

Working outside the city brings with it another imperative, simultaneously ecological and political. Rural land is in a constant state of flux, but as cities have grown in the modern period, the

Stan Allen Architect, Peter Saul Studio,
Germantown, NY, 2014

Stan Allen Architect, E/V House & Studio,
Elizaville, NY, 2016

dominant trajectory has been toward development and expansion. The explosion of suburbs in the postwar period consumed vast quantities of land, and changes in transportation and communication technology have enabled the development of more and more remote sites. There is no clear demarcation today between country and city, which means rethinking what it means to build on previously undeveloped land. All of the global forces at work in cities—finance, technology, communication, resources, and politics—are present in rural sites as well, with the added pressure of protection of the open space. Anytime a site is cleared, something of the common good is lost. If we destroy even a small fragment of nature, we are under an ethical imperative to give something back: to avoid, as far as possible, the violation of the landscape and the spirit of the place that so troubled Loos a hundred years ago.

The work presented here does not celebrate the isolated object in a pristine landscape. In many cases, these projects are additions to existing buildings or *outbuildings* that consolidate already developed sites. This is also implicit in the idea of the situated object: modest interventions that create intricate local relationships or pockets of density on the exurban landscape. Rather than evoke the villa in a pastoral landscape, these projects recall the accretion over time of houses, barns, and structures on a working farm. These landscapes are already built upon; these projects respond to specific constraints of site and program, but also to a history of lived inhabitation.

To be an architect today requires an odd mix of arrogance and humility. Arrogance to take responsibility for a large, complicated, and expensive piece of work; humility to understand that architecture's logic and consistency come not from an individual but from the shared knowledge of the discipline and a collective understanding of buildings and places. Architecture is both in and of the world, and architects are uniquely positioned to transform that reality. But architecture changes the world slowly and incrementally, and works by definition locally and not globally.

Stan Allen, April 2020

Stan Allen Architect, L/B Studio, Roanoke, VA, 2018. Photo: Stan Allen

OUT

INGS

BUILD

"I use the word 'naive' in its peri-mathematical sense, as one speaks of the naive theory of sets. We forge ahead without undue refinement. We try to prove motion by walking."

Raymond Queneau

"Genius is the error in the system."

Paul Klee

Venturi and Rauch, Trubeck and Wislocki Houses, Nantucket Island, MA, 1971

Stan Allen Architect, K/S Library, Milan, NY, 2018

Design Rules

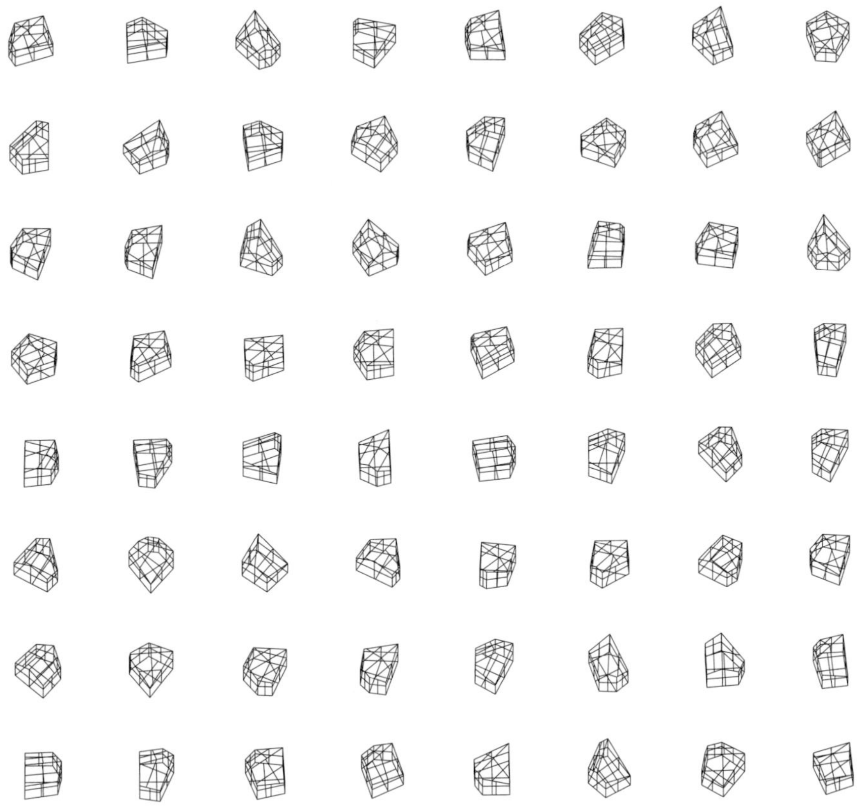

Array of design iterations: specific objects

Architectural knowledge is cumulative. Programs and building types repeat over time, and history offers a reservoir of solutions that form a starting point for future work. One way to achieve consistency across a body of work is simply to respect the logic of the discipline. As Adolf Loos observed, there is no need to reinvent the roof. In each of these projects, familiar forms appear in unfamiliar relationships.

But there is also a more individual identity that a body of work acquires. Just as the discipline moves forward as a conversation with its past, an architect builds a body of work on past work. The work presented here employs formal strategies and design techniques that have emerged in buildings and projects developed over the past ten years. Specifically, they are shaped by three consistent design strategies: a formal language that works with ordinary building materials; the iconic potential of the figural roofline; and a working process based on simple rules, which in turn implies a serial attitude.

ORDINARY BUILDING

More than the shaping of raw materials, building today is largely a matter of assembling a series of pre-made elements on site. Doors, windows, hardware, roofing, and siding are all ordered from a catalog. Standardized framing lumber has a logic of assembly dictated by codes, tools, and convention. The architect and the builder work with these standardized construction systems, making incremental changes to meet the needs of the project and the logics of the place. These projects accept this language of ordinary building technology. They are not driven by invention, but instead accept these fundamentally modern conditions of standardization and normalization. They work with simple, readily available technologies: lightweight wood framing, wood or fiber-cement siding, metal roofing, standardized doors and windows. As in American vernacular building, this lends itself to a language of taut, compact objects with minimal eaves and overhangs: a language of singular objects rather than complex assemblies of parts. Their realization is less a matter of craft and more a matter of know-how, workmanship, and rules of thumb. I like this simple, unheroic way of building. It belongs to a community of knowledge, perhaps not organically embedded in a shared local culture—as Loos imagined the artisan builder could be—but for the realities of the present, the best we can hope for. And in its own way, it is democratic and readily accessible.

Pl. 28.

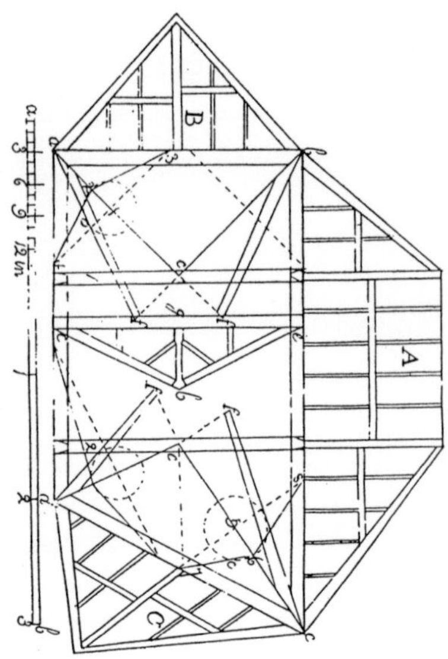

Plan of a roof in ledgments, from Asher Benjamin, *The Country Builder's Assistant*, 1797

Stan Allen Architect, Peter Saul Studio; framing under construction

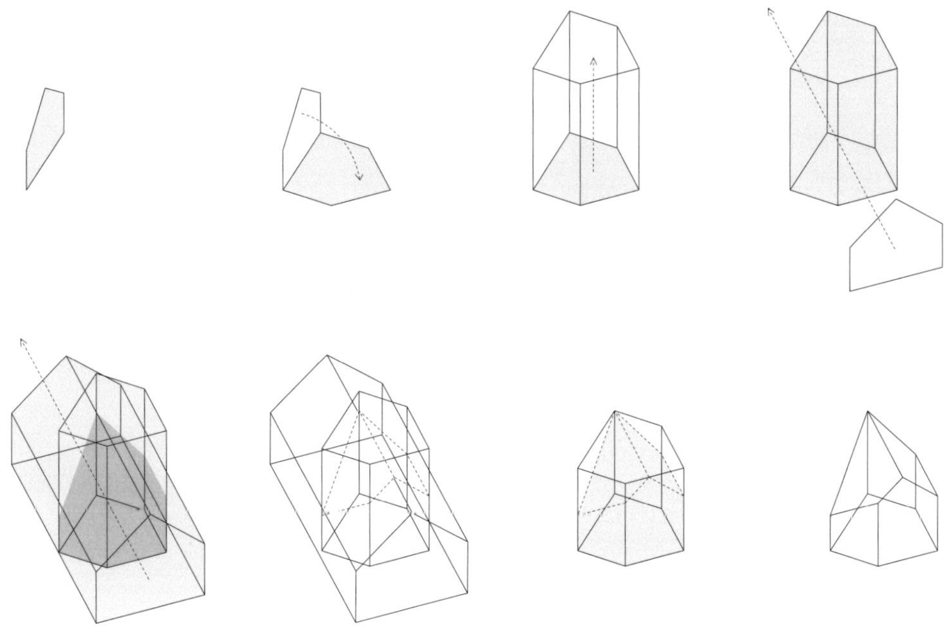

Stan Allen Architect, E/V House & Studio, diagram of design procedures

Working with these ordinary building materials means that, in large part, what unifies the work presented here is a shared set of design procedures. The process consists of establishing a few simple variables and a set of operative rules that configure a working design model. The goal is a simple—but not reductive—object. A good rule set has to be flexible enough to accommodate difference without compromising its internal logic, but clear and robust enough to structure a legible body of work. Decisions are always made one step removed from the material. The design process is not linear, but iterative, with never more than three or four steps to each iteration. I like that immediacy. The accrued knowledge of the problem means that the solutions, which always resemble one another, become more refined and specific over time.

The use of a consistent rule set to generate forms moves away from the specific toward the general. In each individual iteration there are other versions implied, even if not literally present. The E/V Studio, for example, can be a freestanding building or a repeated element in a f in a field-like array. The plan figures are always open and incomplete. In both the singular and aggregate variations, the formal solution has a provisional character: because the geometries are not final and self-evident, they suggest that any instance is but one of many possible configurations.

Stan Allen Architect, array of paper study models, 2016

Wood teaching models of crystal forms, Germany, c. 1890

Stan Allen Architect, E/V House & Studio; study models, 2015

SHED ROOF

These projects all work with the figural and expressive character of the roof as a primal architectural element signifying ritual, shelter, and collective assembly. The pitched roof simultaneously recalls primitive hut and Doric temple, garden shed and Monopoly piece, or a child's drawing of a house. It is easy to build and highly efficient at shedding water. The symbolic and pragmatic coincide; but examined objectively, the pitched roof is simply an abstract geometric figure: an extruded triangle. In the E/V Studio and related projects, a simple pitched roof is misaligned with the five-sided plan figure, producing unexpected intersections; in the L/B Studio and the Ghost Shed, multiple elemental roof forms are embedded in a single figure. There are exceptions: the J/S House is a simple flat-roofed cube, in deference to the repeated peaks of the original house. The overall complex conserves the figural energy of the original house.

Stan Allen Architect, J/S House, Gallatin, NY, 2018

1. M/M HOUSE & STUDIO

In 2001, I designed a modest one-story house on a five-acre wooded lot in the Hudson Highlands for a well-known artist and her husband. Ten years later, the same clients approached us with a new brief: add a working studio to the existing house. The original house is organized as an open loft space with services concentrated in a compact central block, allowing for natural cross-ventilation and flexible living space. Responding to the constraints of the sloping site, the house is oriented to capture light and views. The studio is a vertical counterpoint to the horizontal body of the existing house. Light enters from a tall clerestory, and windows are minimized to ensure generous wall space. The studio is inward-looking, separated from the living space yet inflected by site conditions and working requirements. The five-sided plan figure gives a subtle dynamic to this functional workspace.

This second phase was also an opportunity to implement a new landscape strategy. Working closely with the landscape architects, we created a structured geometric frame for the house, which contrasts with the naturalistic character of the larger site. Within the courtyard precinct is a carefully tended succulent garden; outside that line, native plants and a natural topography prevail. The space between the house and studio becomes an extended foyer, which frames the courtyard space and serves as a semipublic space for receptions and exhibitions.

Stan Allen Architect, M/M House & Studio

Stan Allen Architect,
E/V House & Studio

2. E/V HOUSE & STUDIO

Situated on a rural site in the Hudson River Valley, the property includes barns, outbuildings, and a former hunting lodge converted for residential use. The project encompasses an addition to the original lodge, and a working architecture studio. In this rural context I wanted to pay homage to the sense of history, place, and local vernacular—not as a nostalgic recall, but to highlight the fundamentally modern character of these compact volumes and simple geometries closely tied to the landscape. The architectural language of the additions is marked by their location in the Hudson River Valley and the legacy of the Hudson River School painters, but also by the site's proximity to New York City: by new technologies of mobility and communication, and by a sense of landscape now seen primarily in motion and in reproduction.

The studio was completed in 2016. The plan is a five-sided figure with a right-angled base that traces out an archetypal house form. This self-imposed constraint, based on past practice, created a series of formal and constructional problems, in particular the geometry of the roof. Projecting up from the five-sided figure and maintaining the profile of the pitched roof (without employing curves or ruled surfaces) produces a family of variations and design options. Each one offers different relationships to site, program, views, and the realities of construction. At this point, the design can be "scripted" in a simple, analog manner. The project for an extension to the original house is an inflected shed with an open plan. Both additions share a material vocabulary of taut wood siding and corrugated metal roofing. The many parts on site resolve into a unified whole, and the similarity of operations creates an unforced consistency over the body of work.

3. L/B STUDIO

This project is located on a wooded lot in the foothills of the Blue Ridge Mountains. The client is a working artist who recently relocated from Los Angeles. She directs an artist residency, and the property functions as a gathering space for visiting artists as well as a painting studio.

Working with the existing topography, we designed an integrated complex of house, studio, and landscaped common spaces. In order to create level ground between the new studio and the existing house, the studio structure itself needed to function as a retaining wall. This dictated the eight-foot-high reinforced concrete wall that forms the perimeter for the studio and courtyard. Lightweight wood framing raises the ceiling height, provides space for insulation, and creates generous wall space in the interior. Natural light enters from skylights on the north pitch of the roofs.

The roof structure is a compound of two pitched-roof volumes, slightly angled in response to the site geometry. This also means that the valley where they intersect slopes naturally for drainage. The iconic profile of the roof repeats at different angles, playing with the recognizability of this familiar vernacular form at the same time as it produces variation and difference.

Stan Allen Architect, L/B Studio

M/M HOUSE & STUDIO

2013

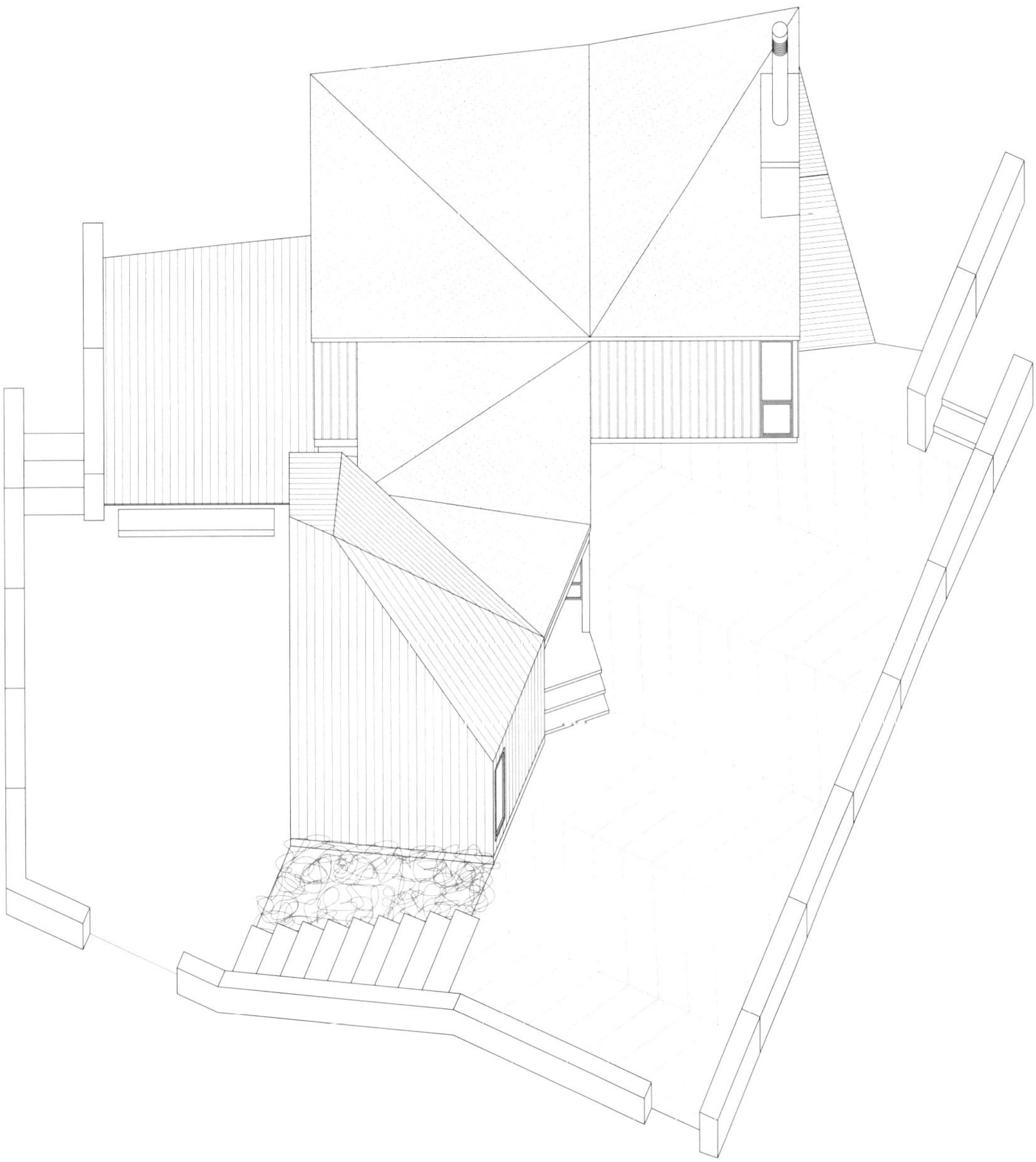

Cold Spring, NY

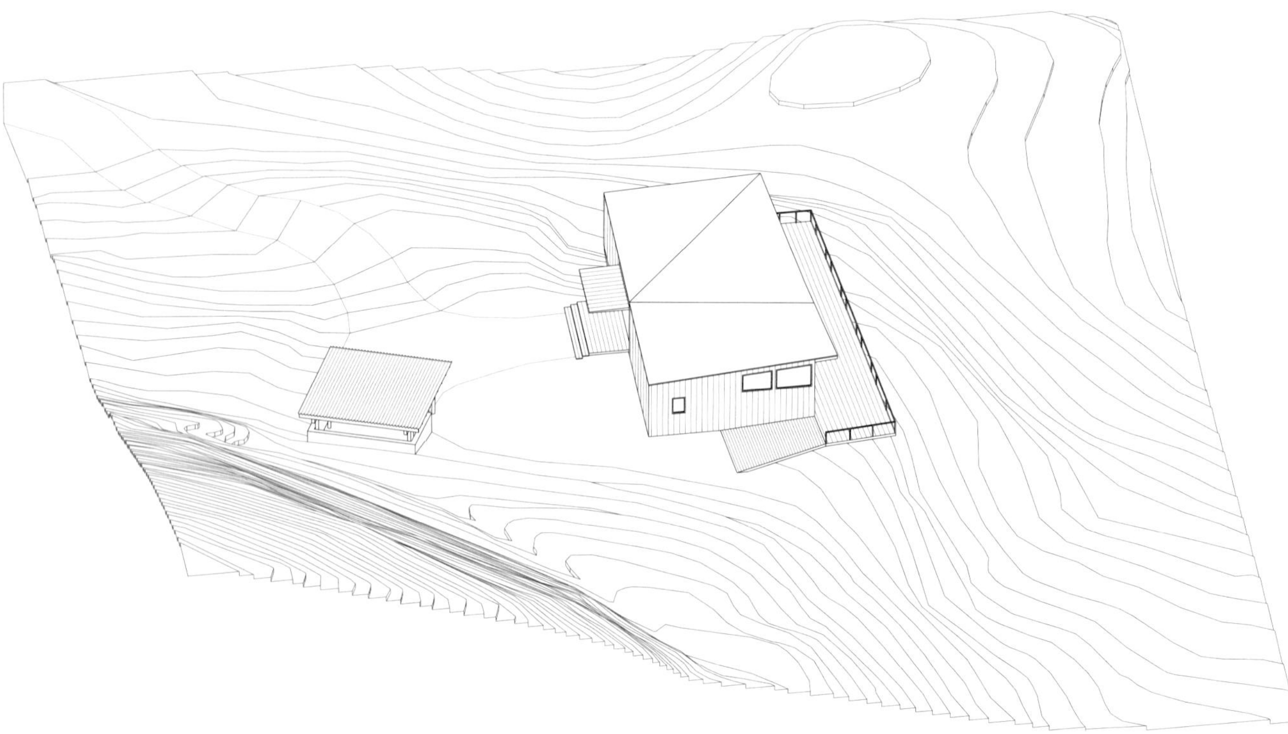

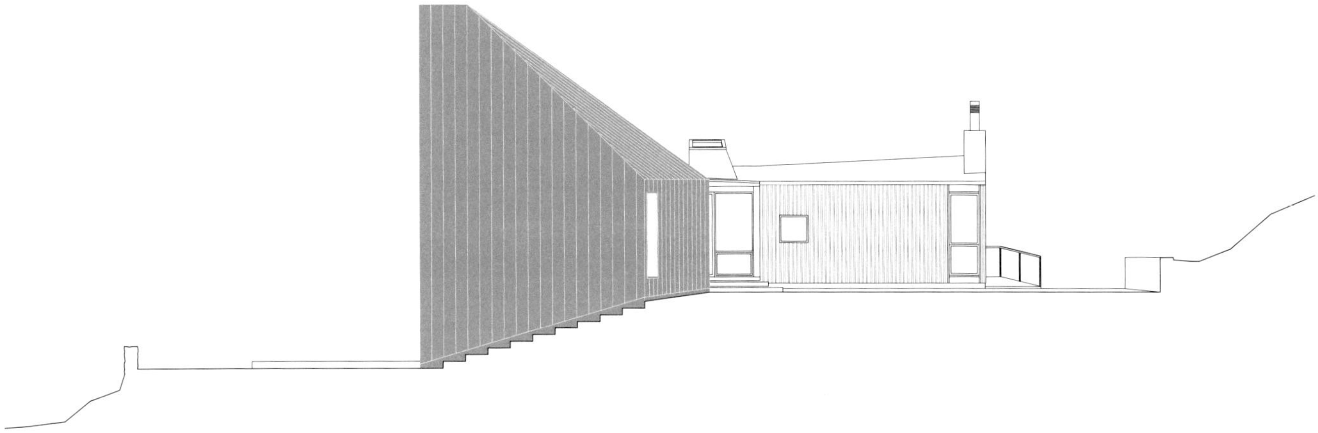

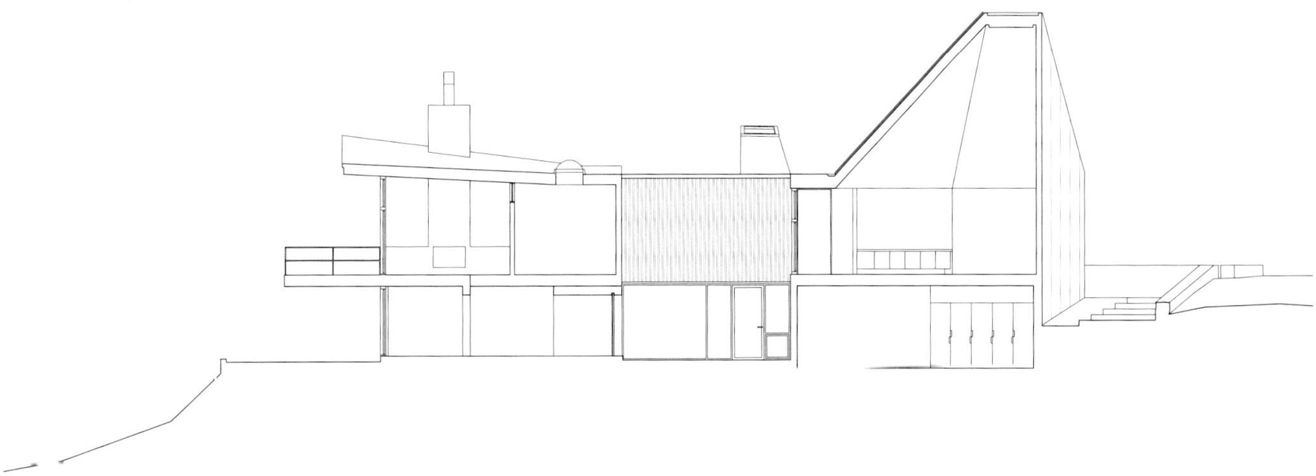

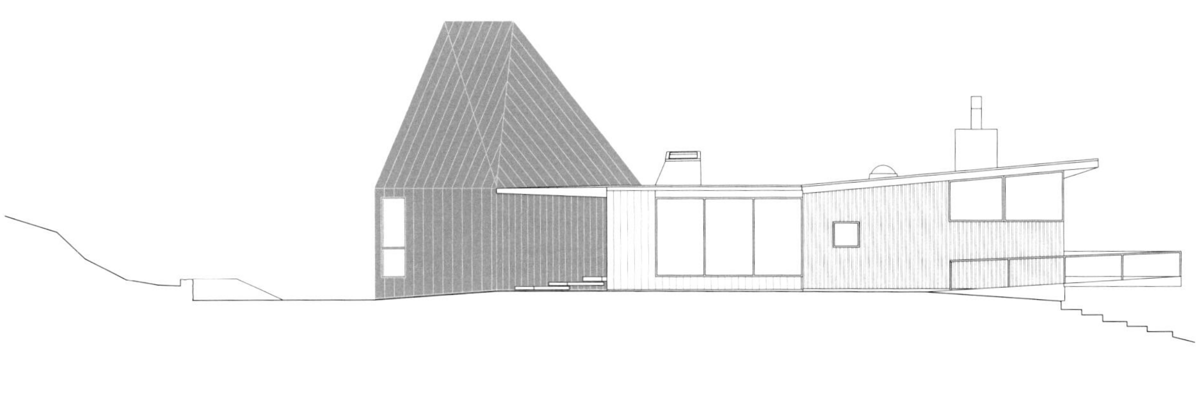

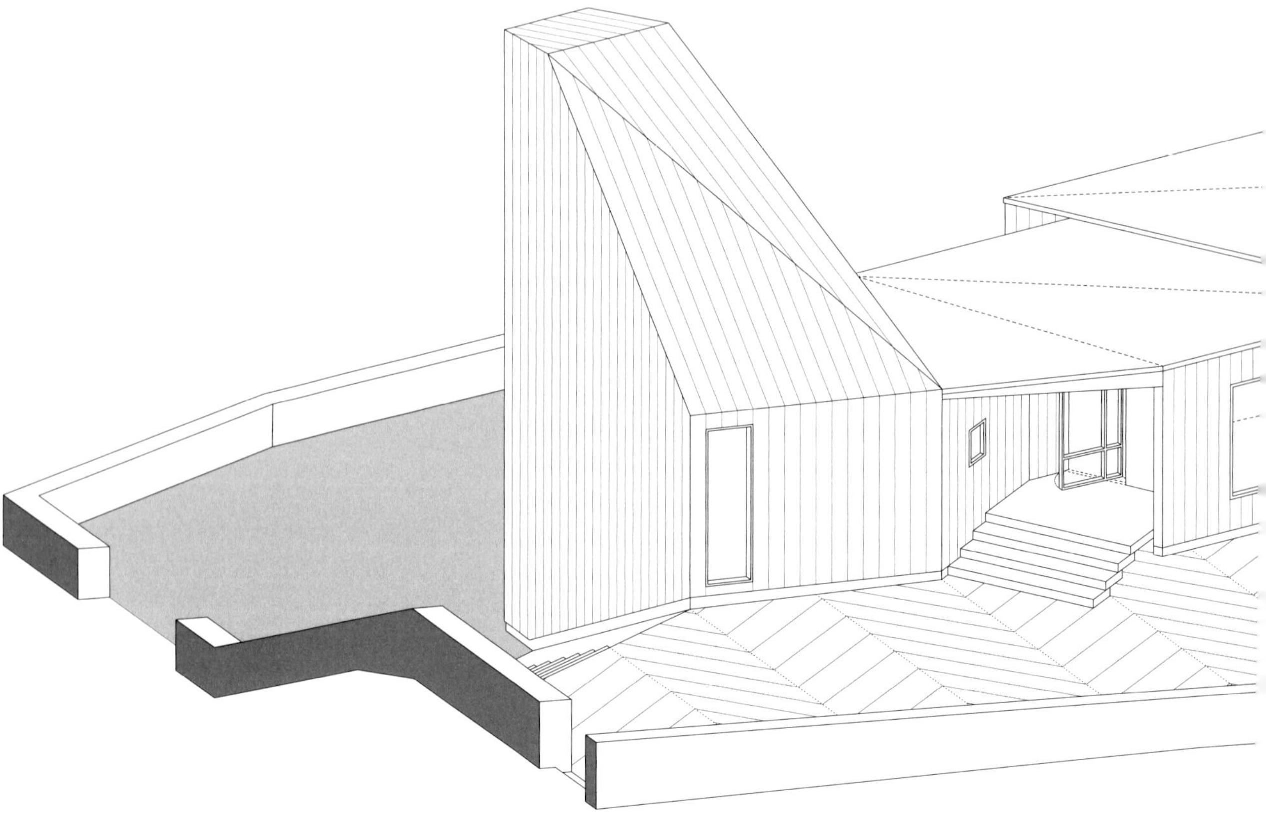

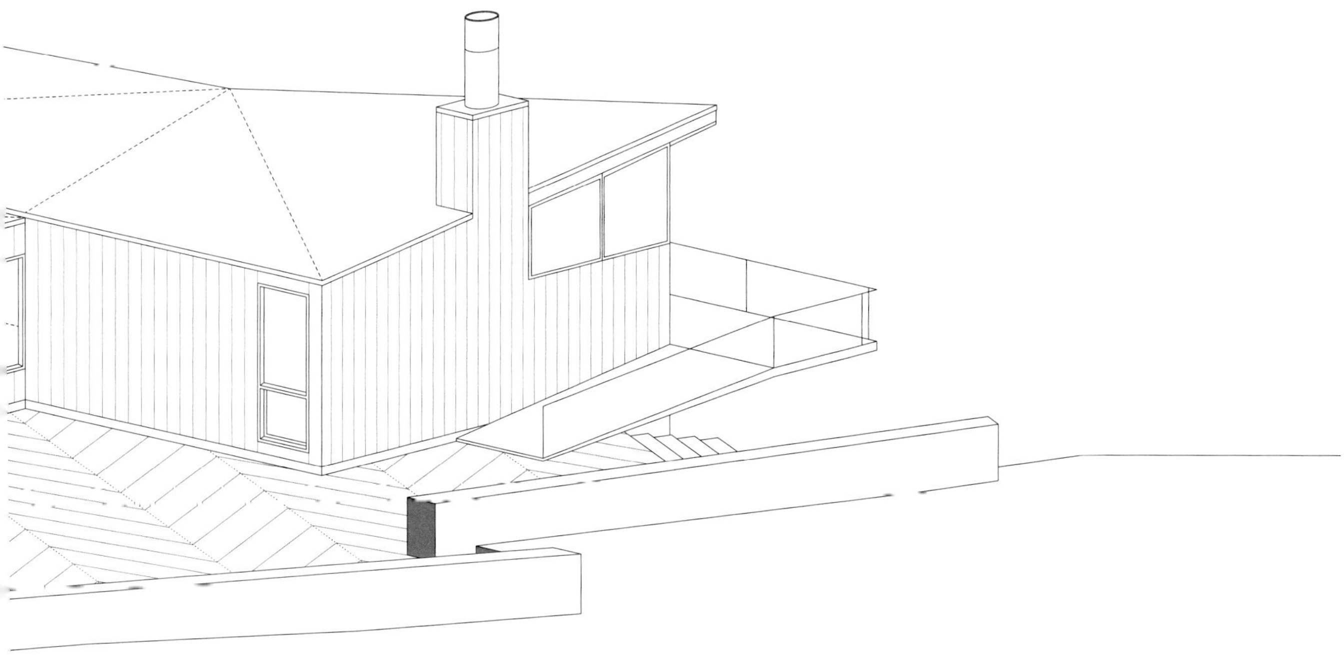

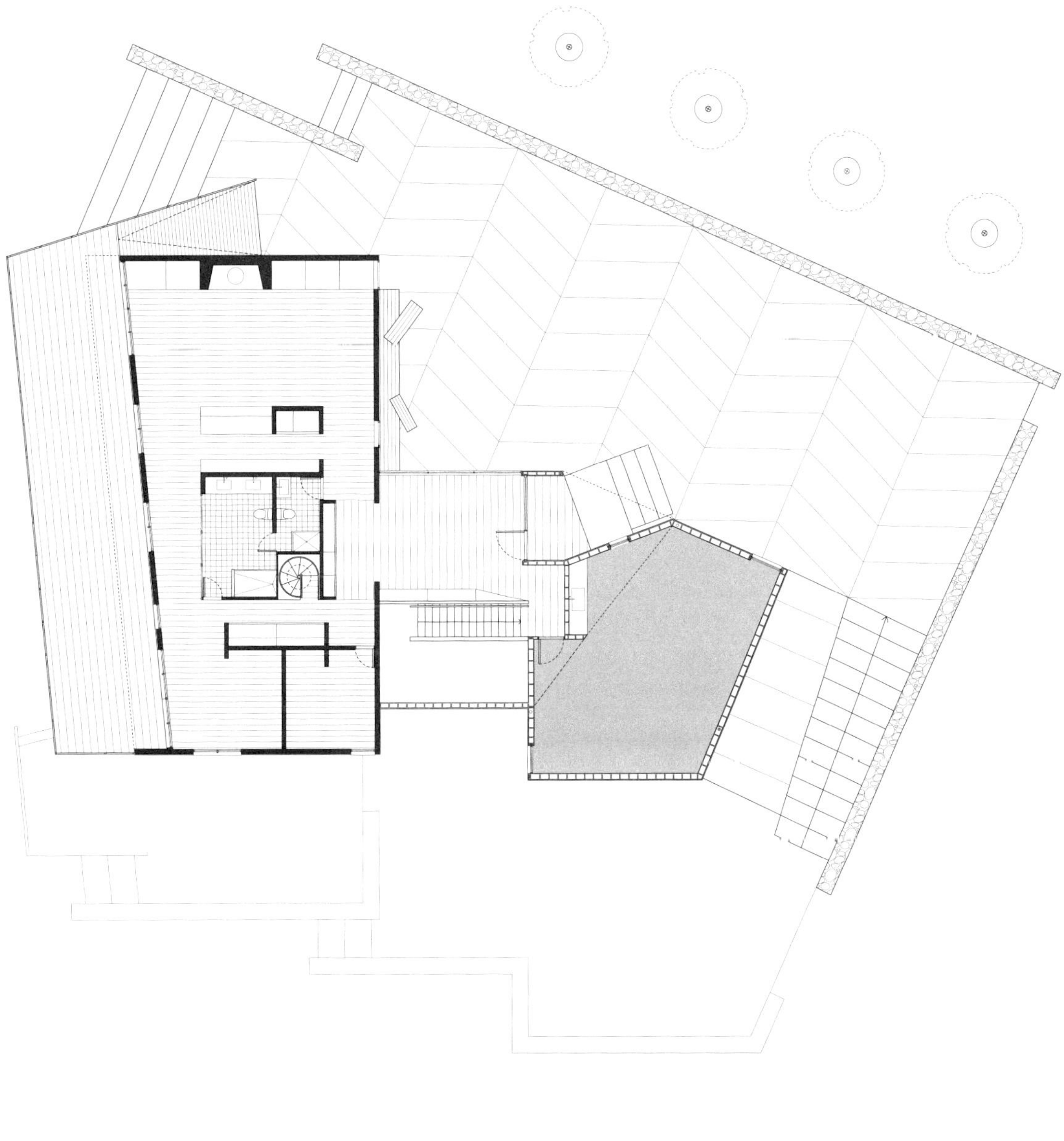

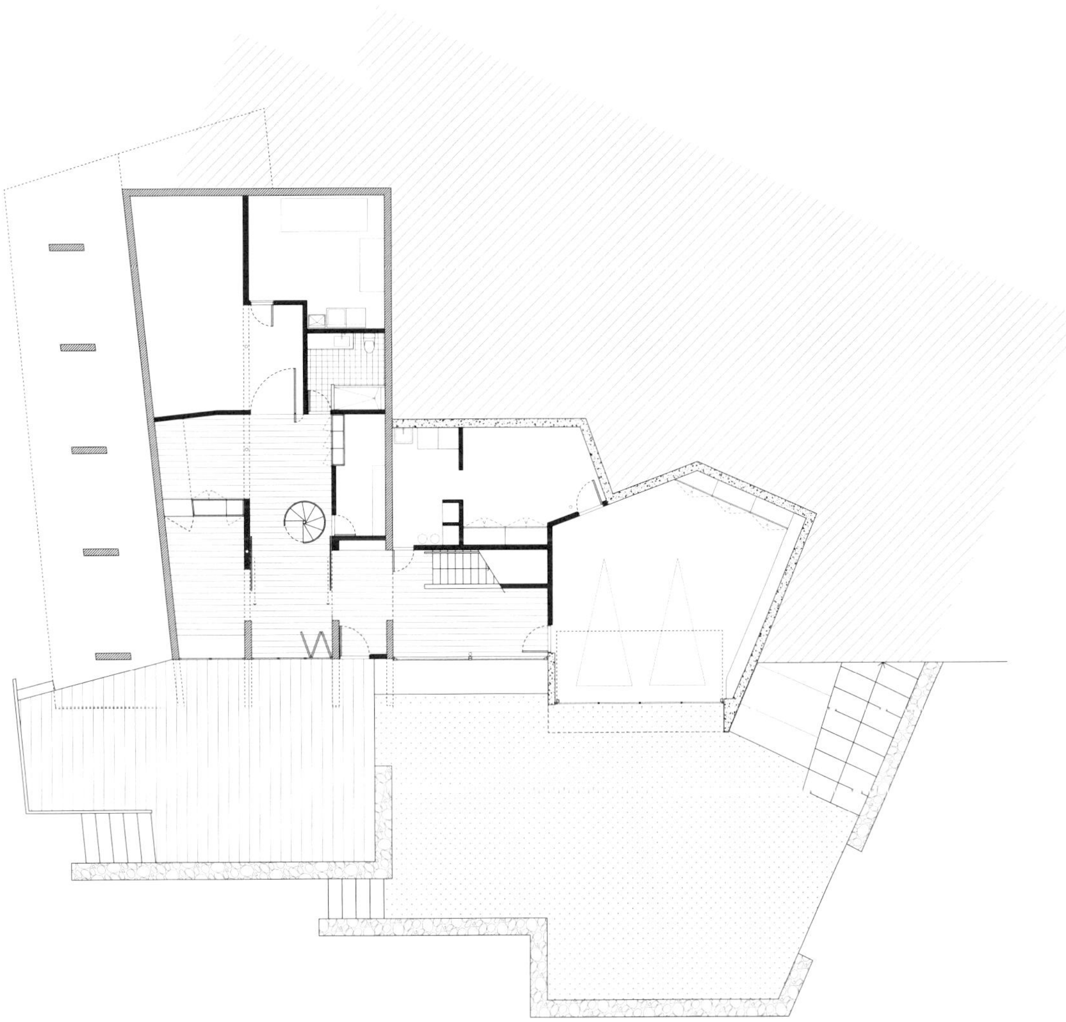

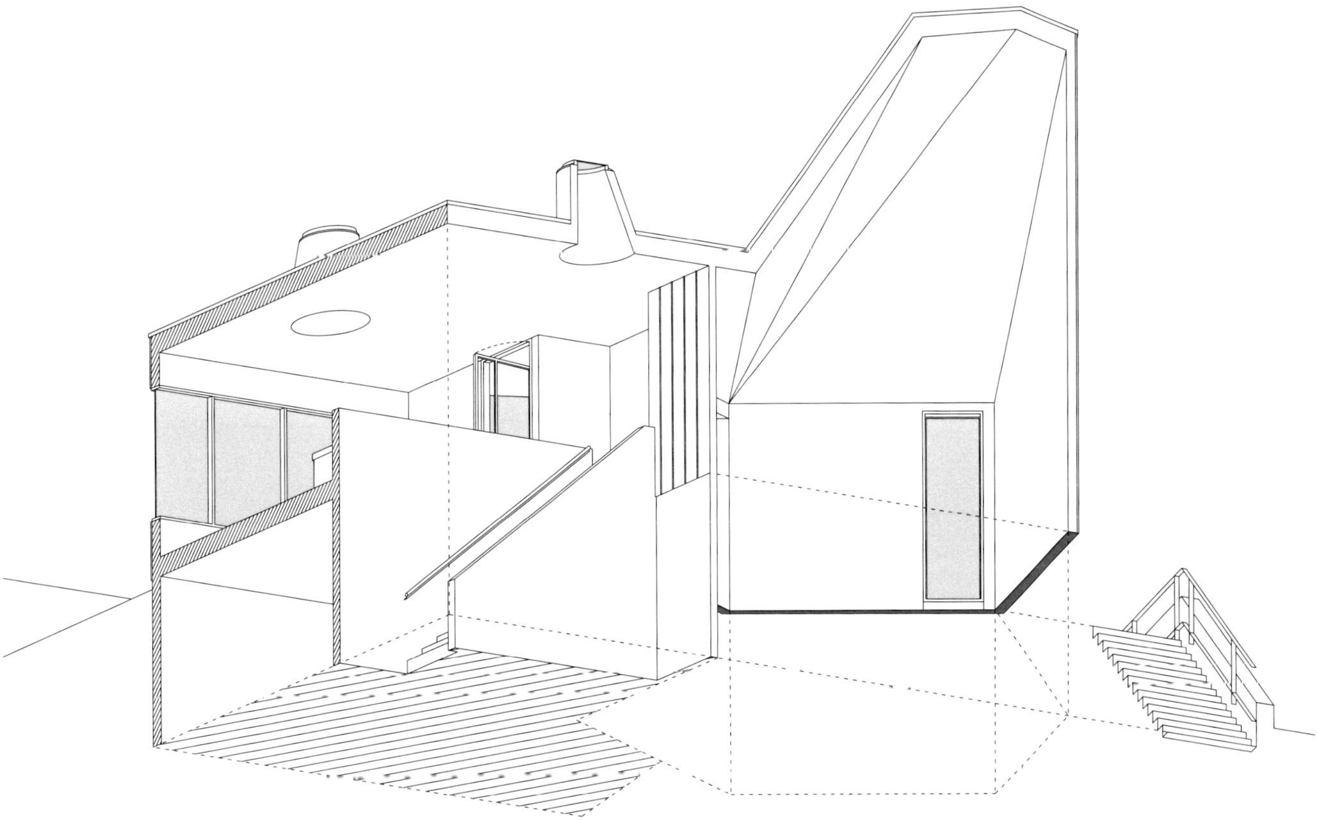

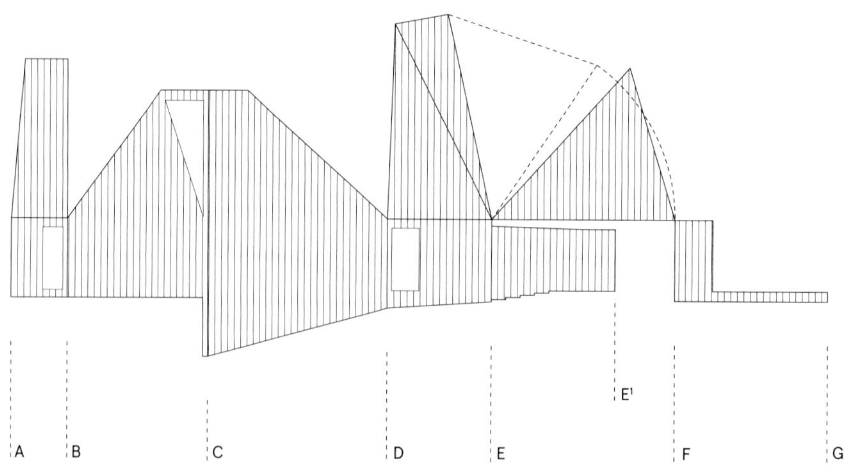
E1
A
B
C
D
E
F
G

FRAGILE

E/V HOUSE & STUDIO

2016/2019

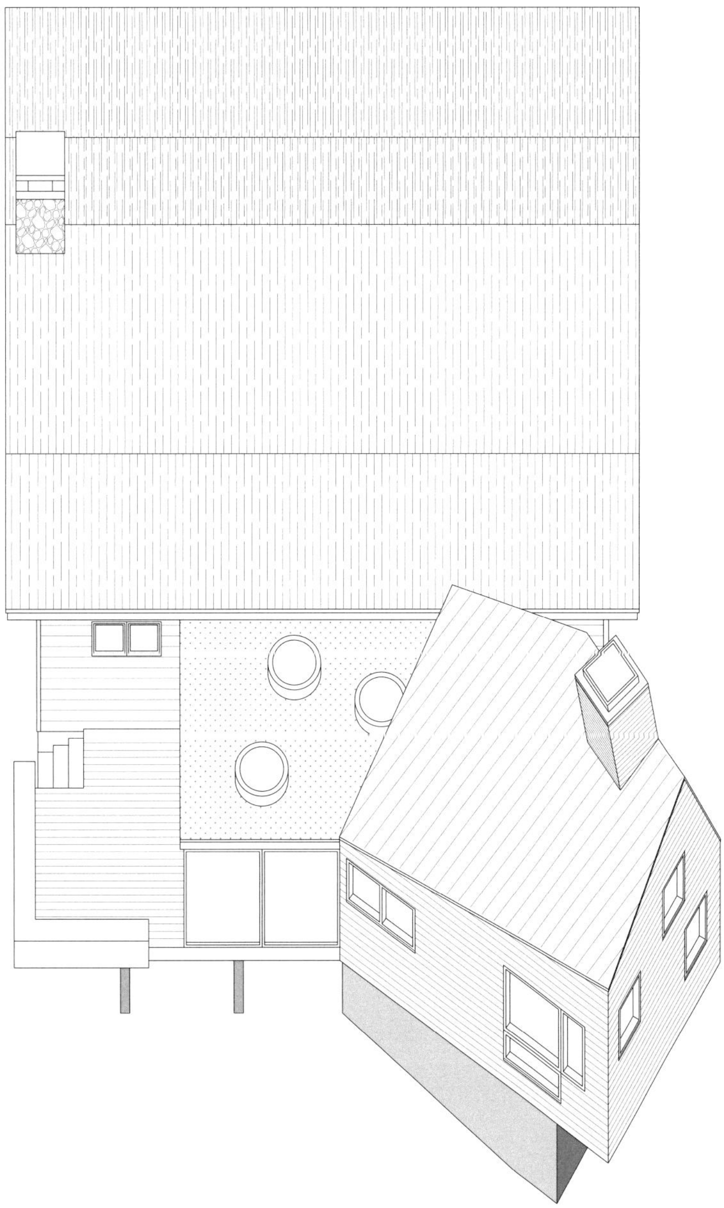

Elizaville, NY

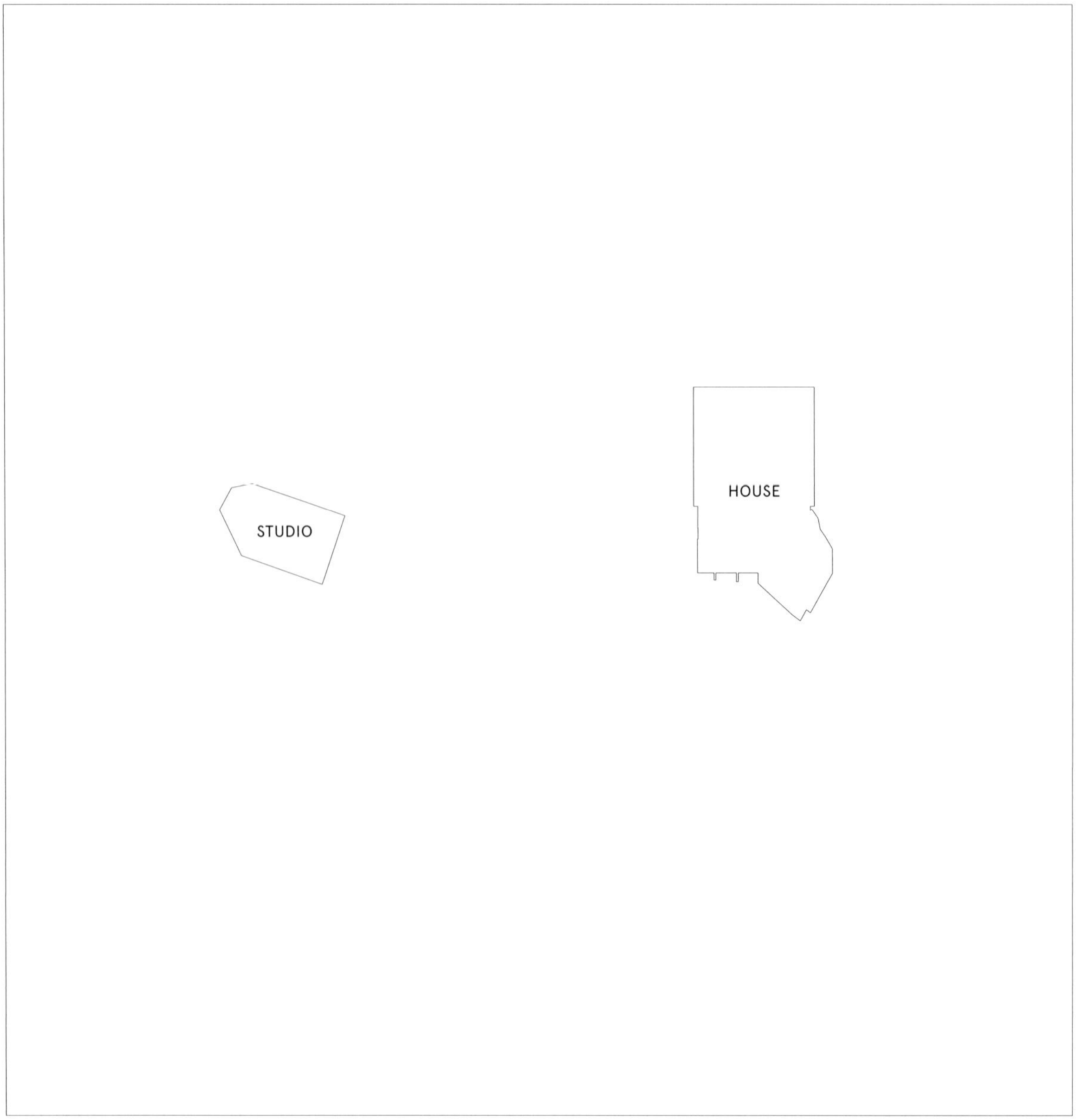
STUDIO
HOUSE

Studio

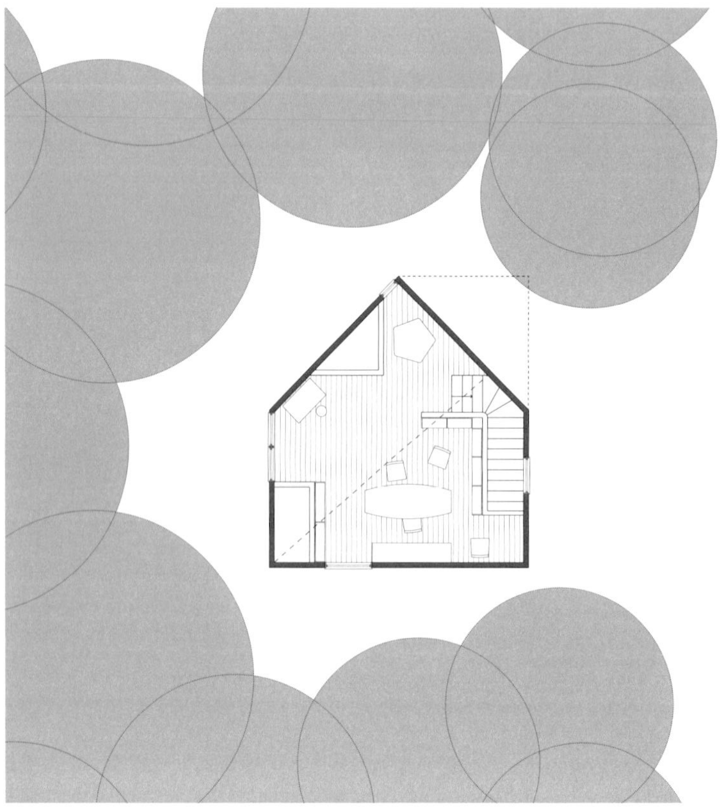

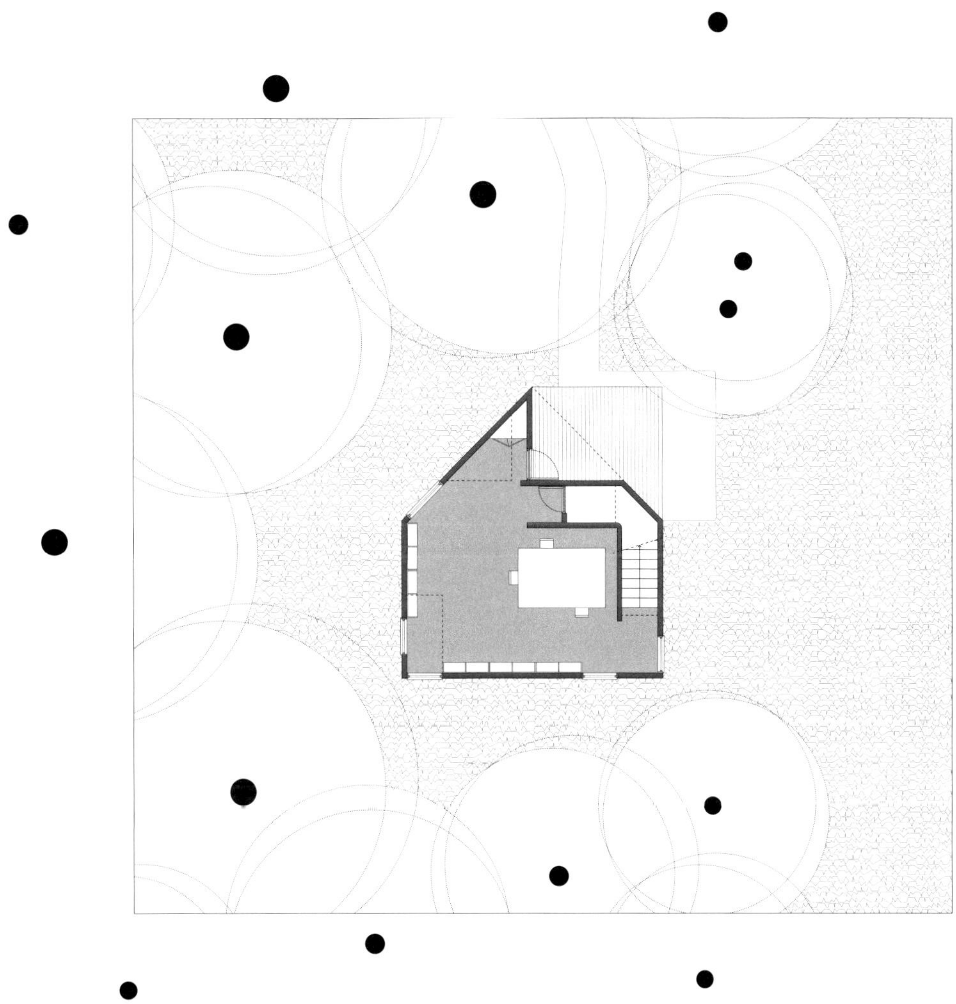

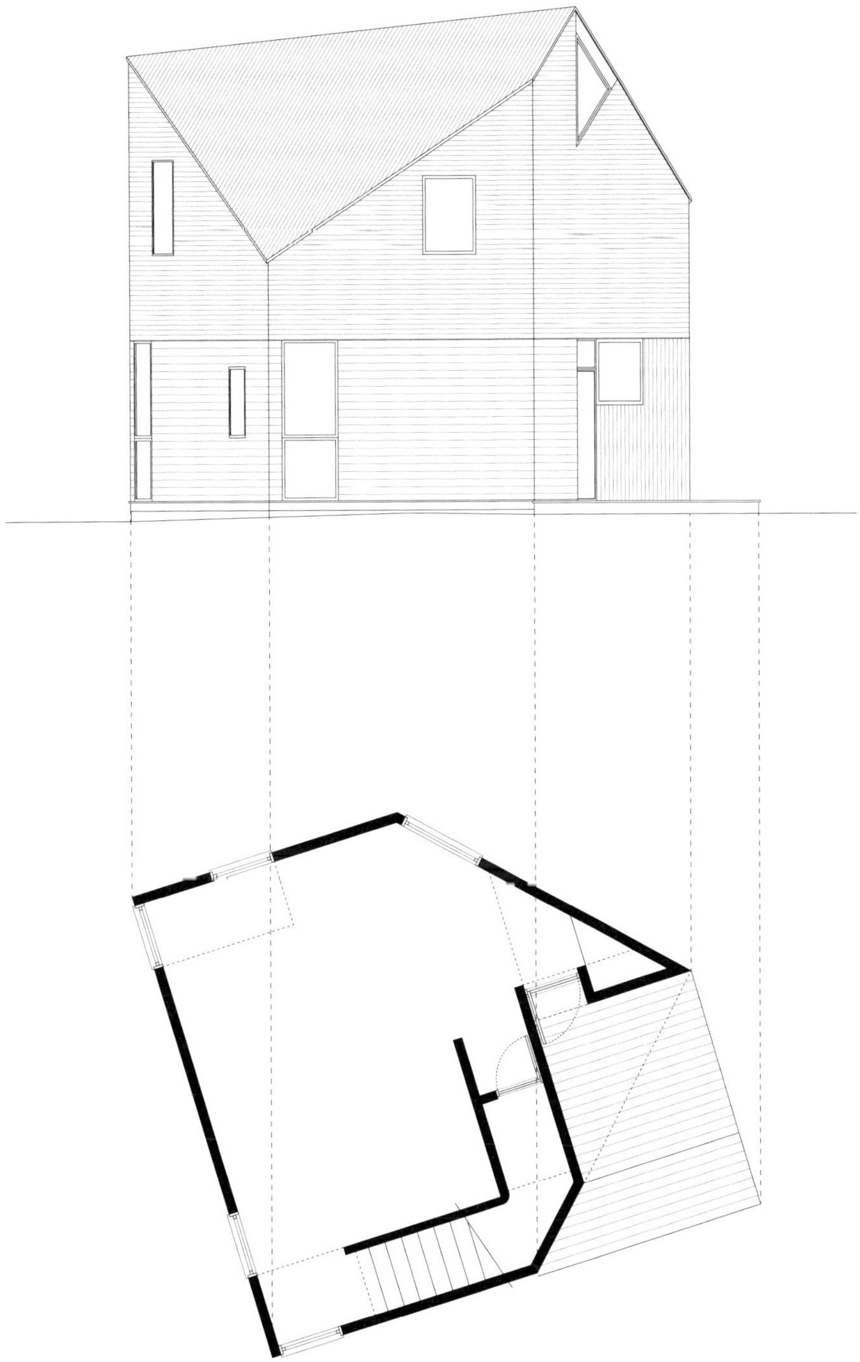

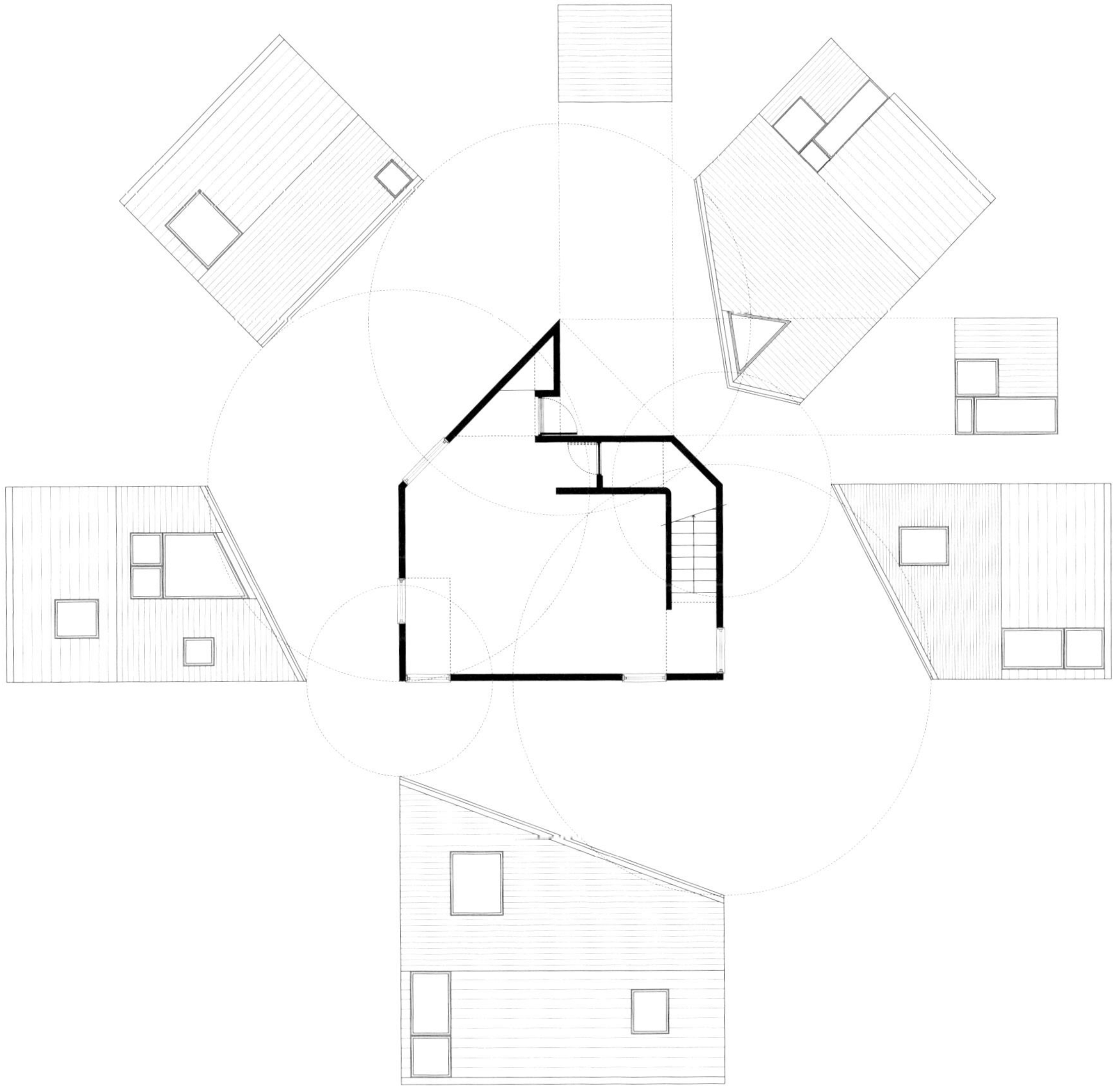

STAN
LEY T
ALLEN

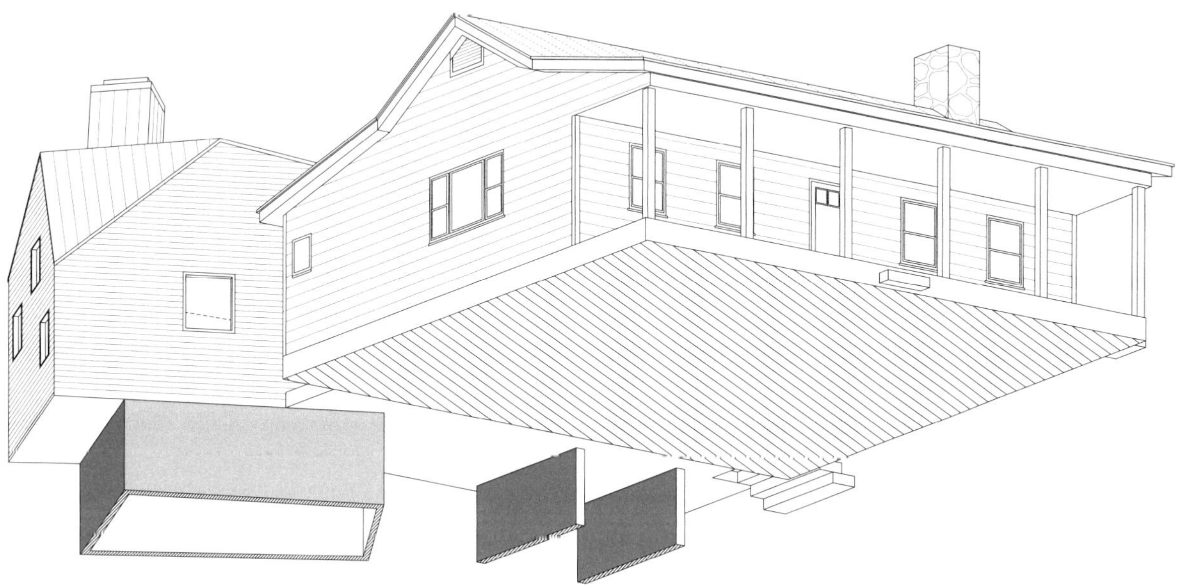

House

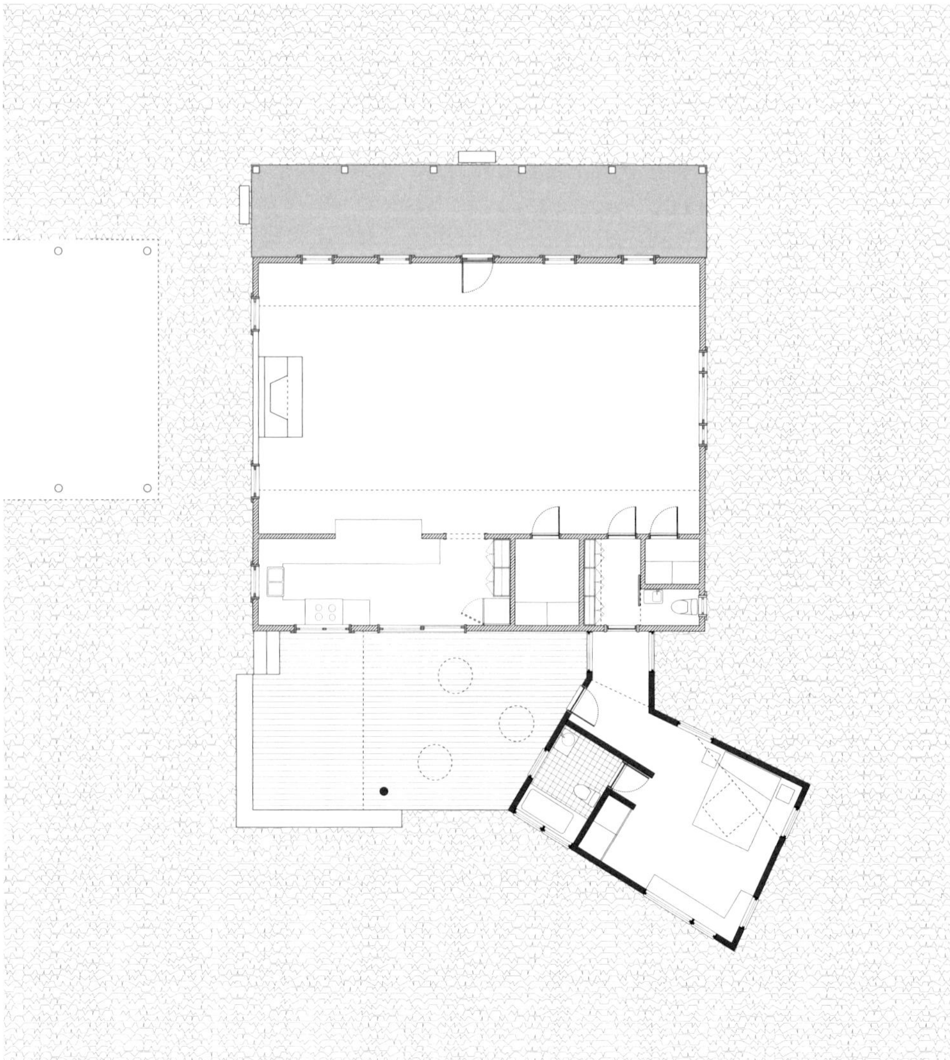

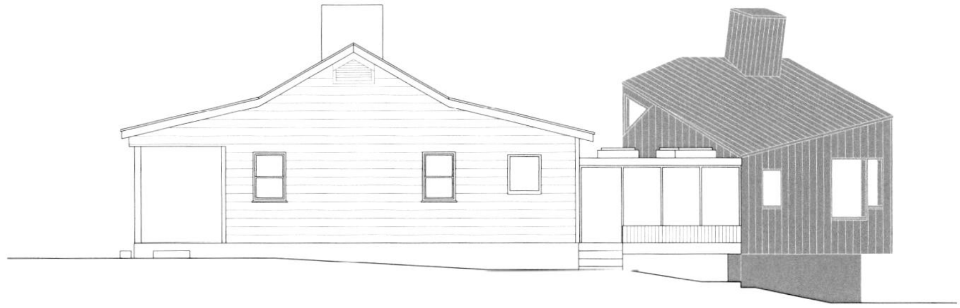

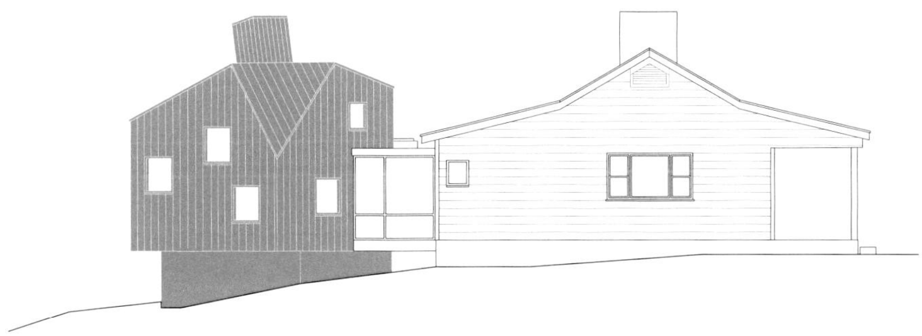

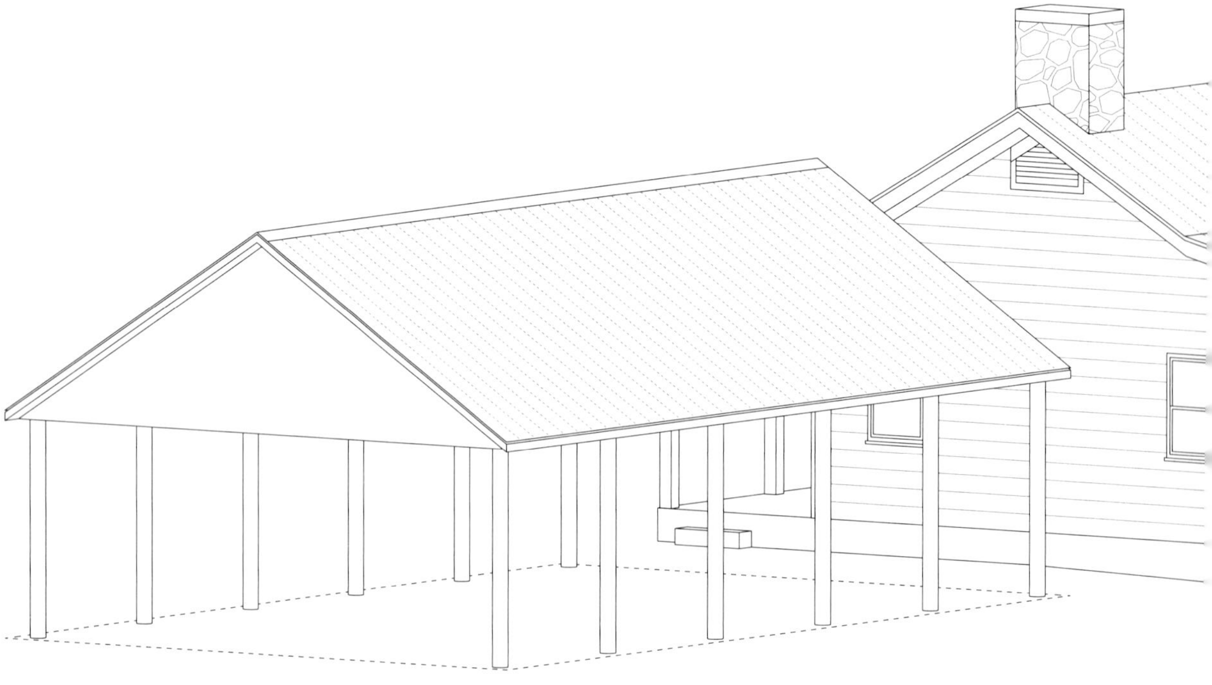

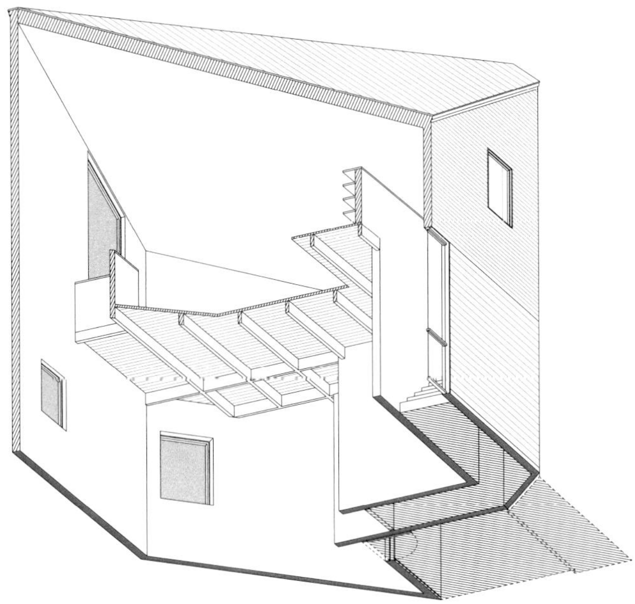

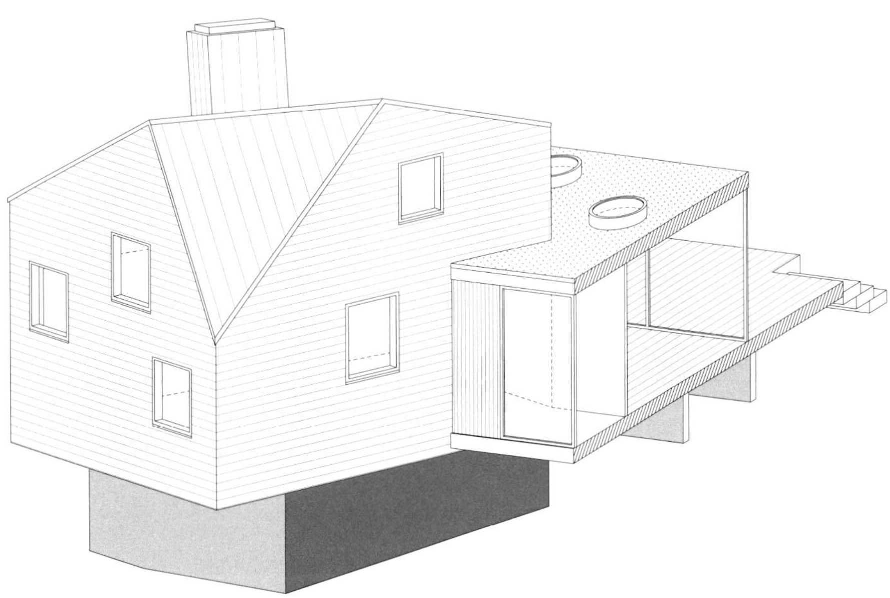

L/B STUDIO

2018

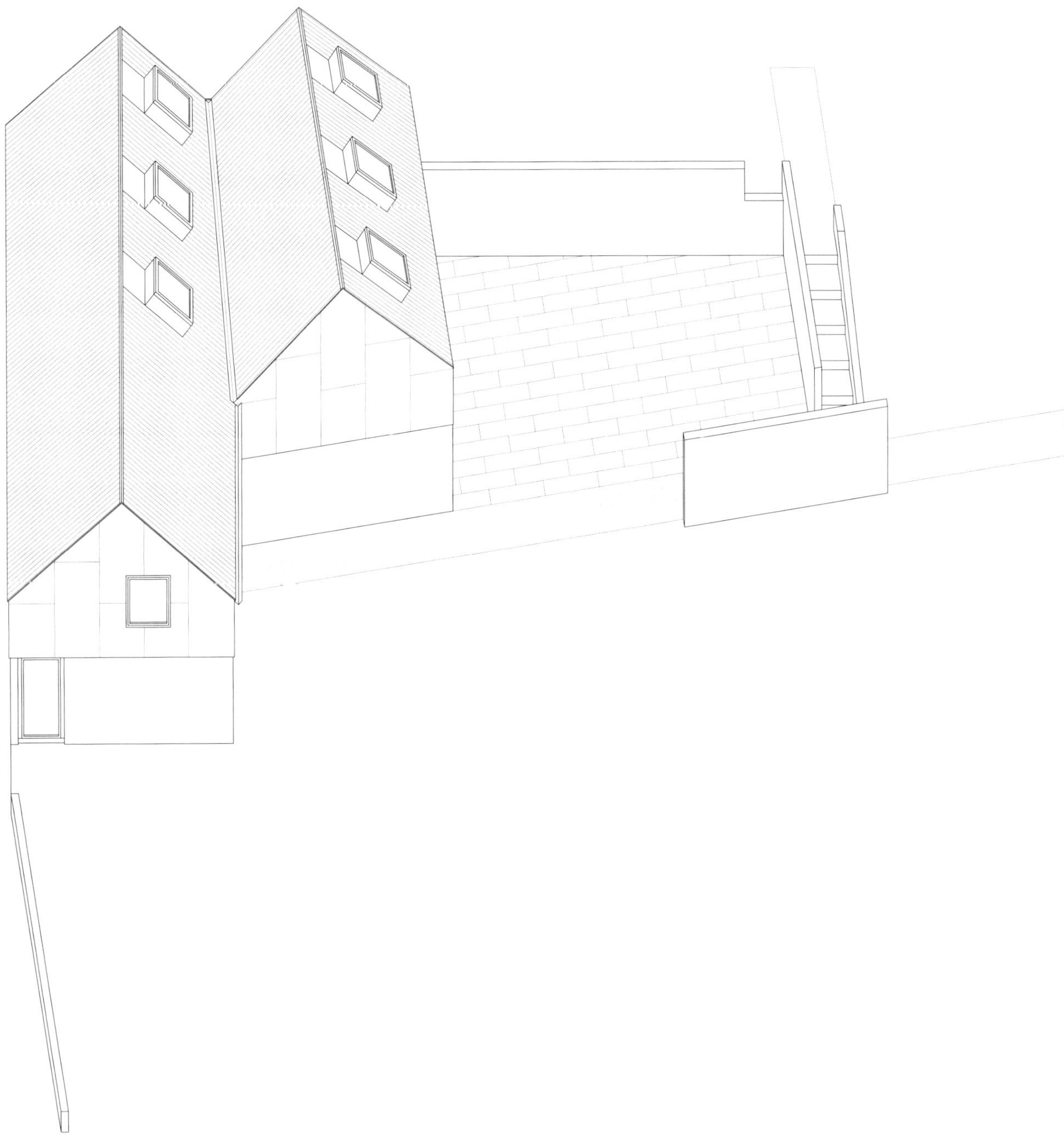

Roanoke, VA

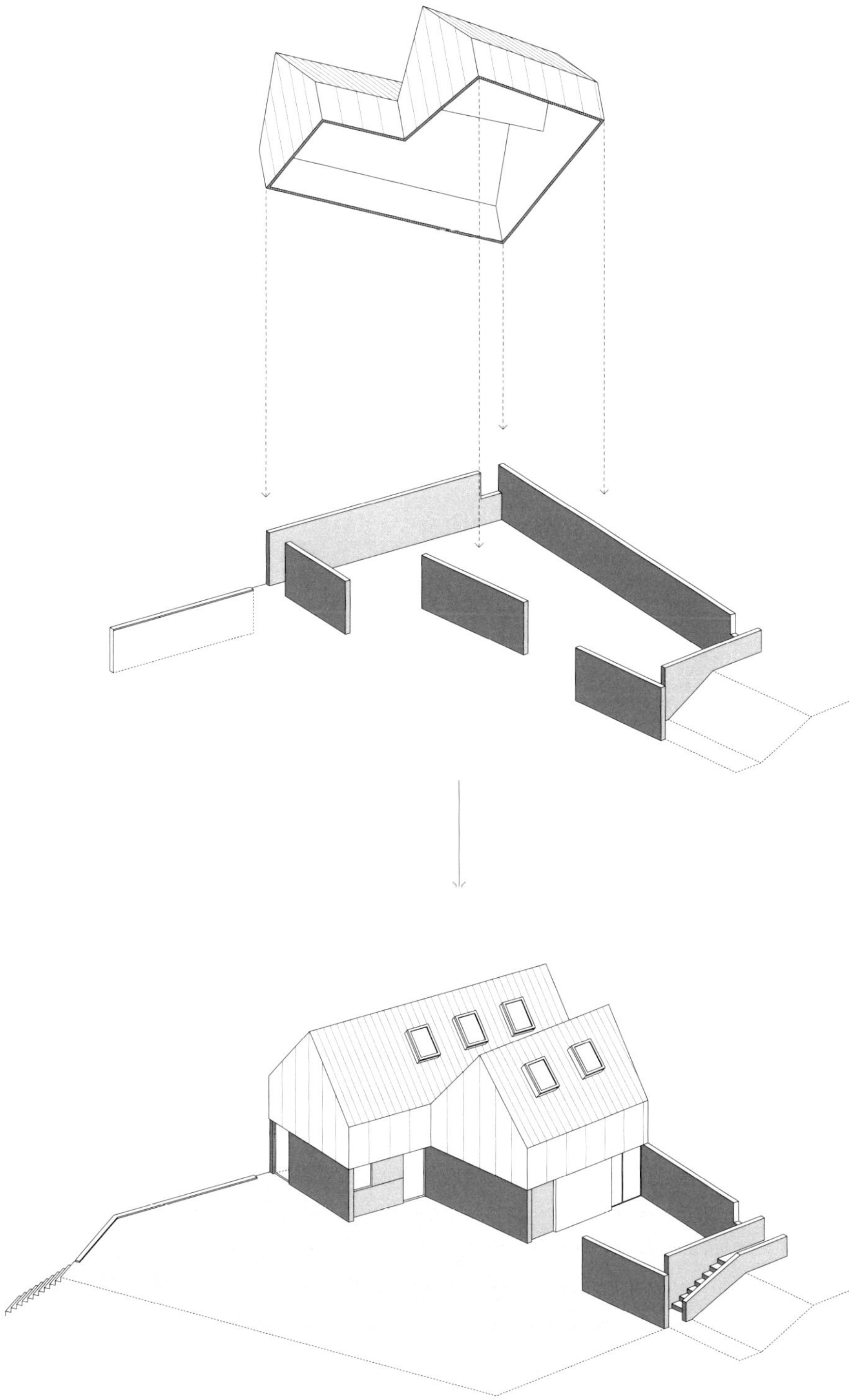

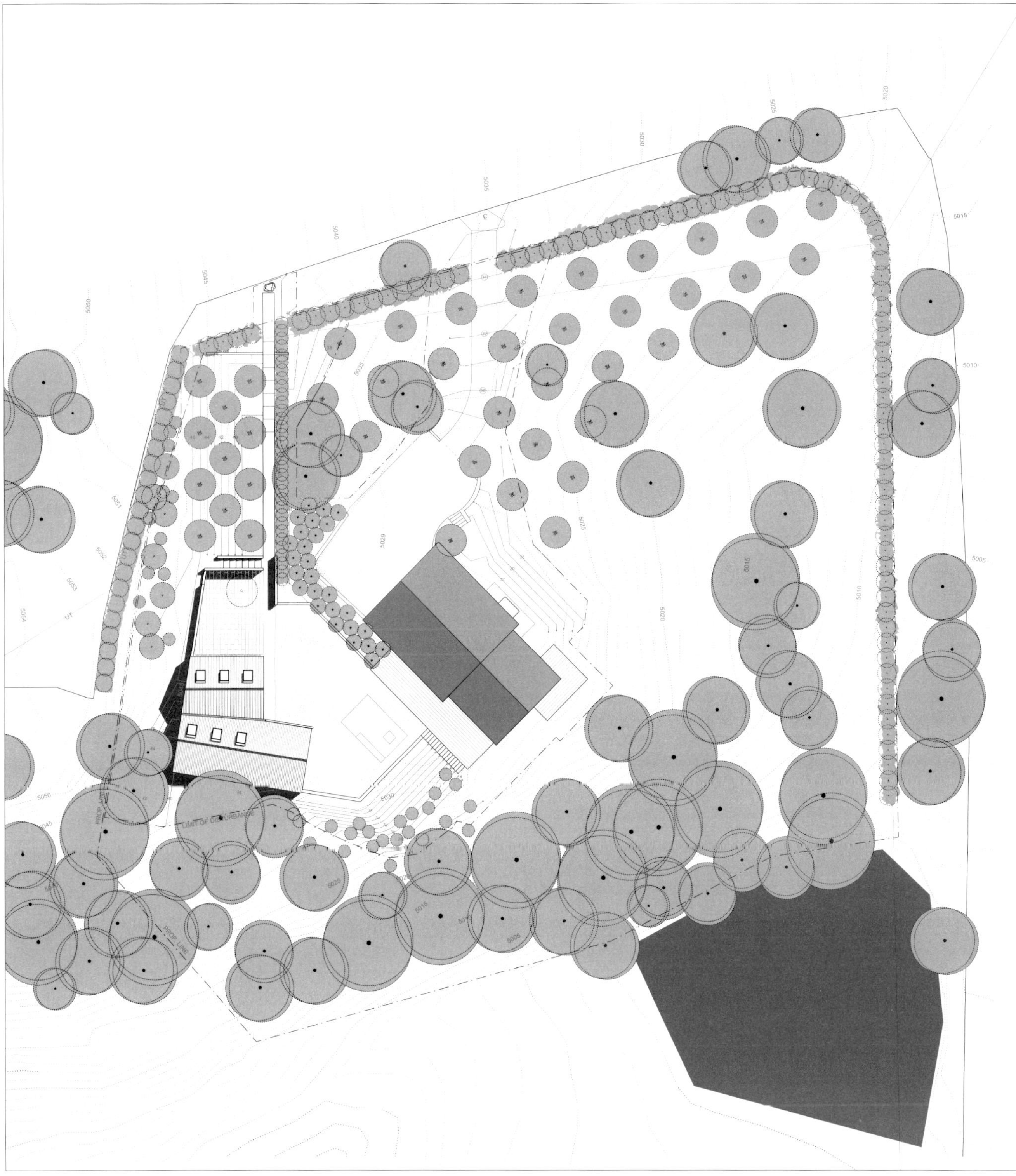

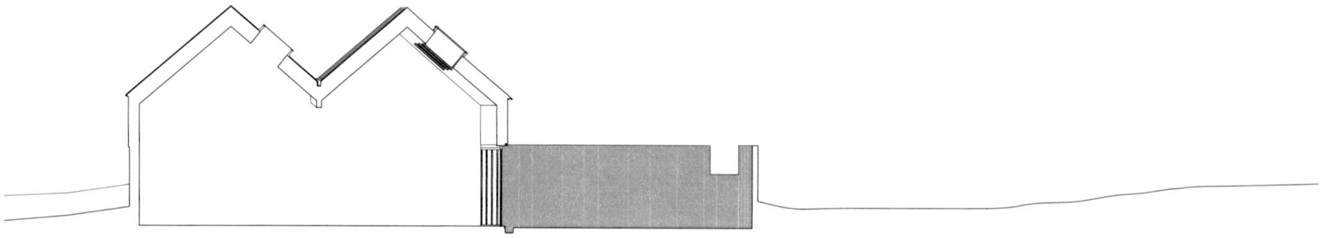

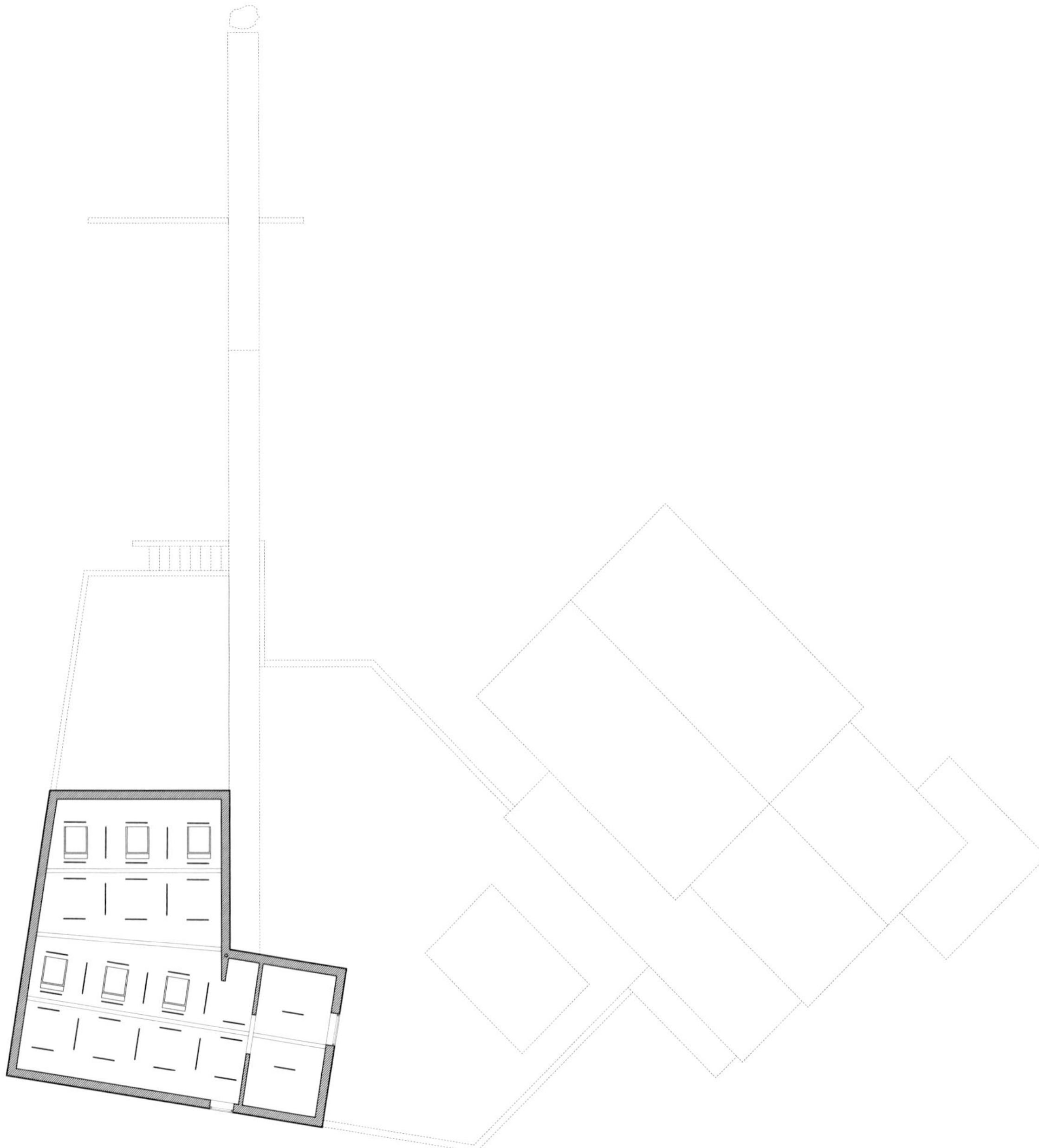

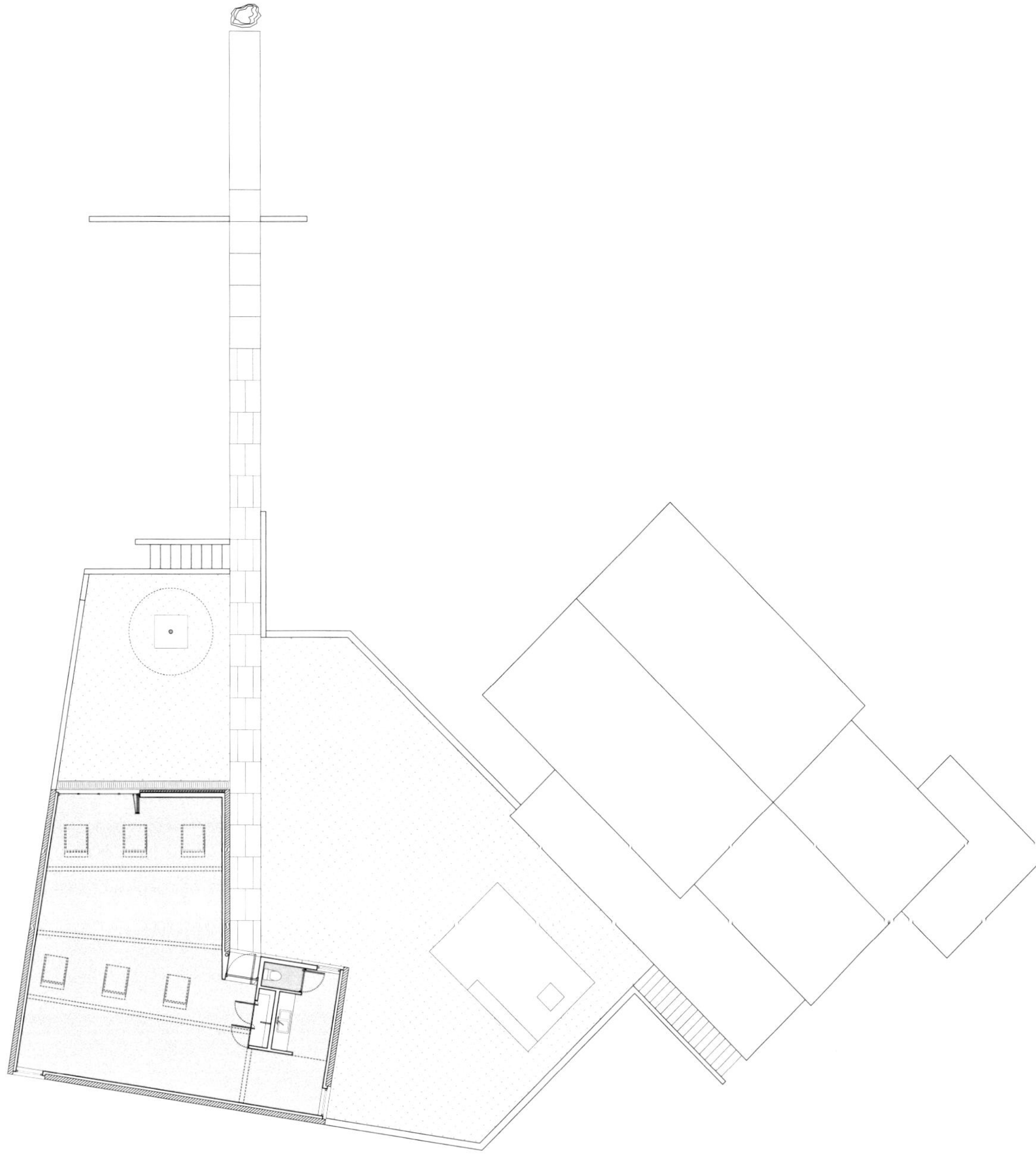

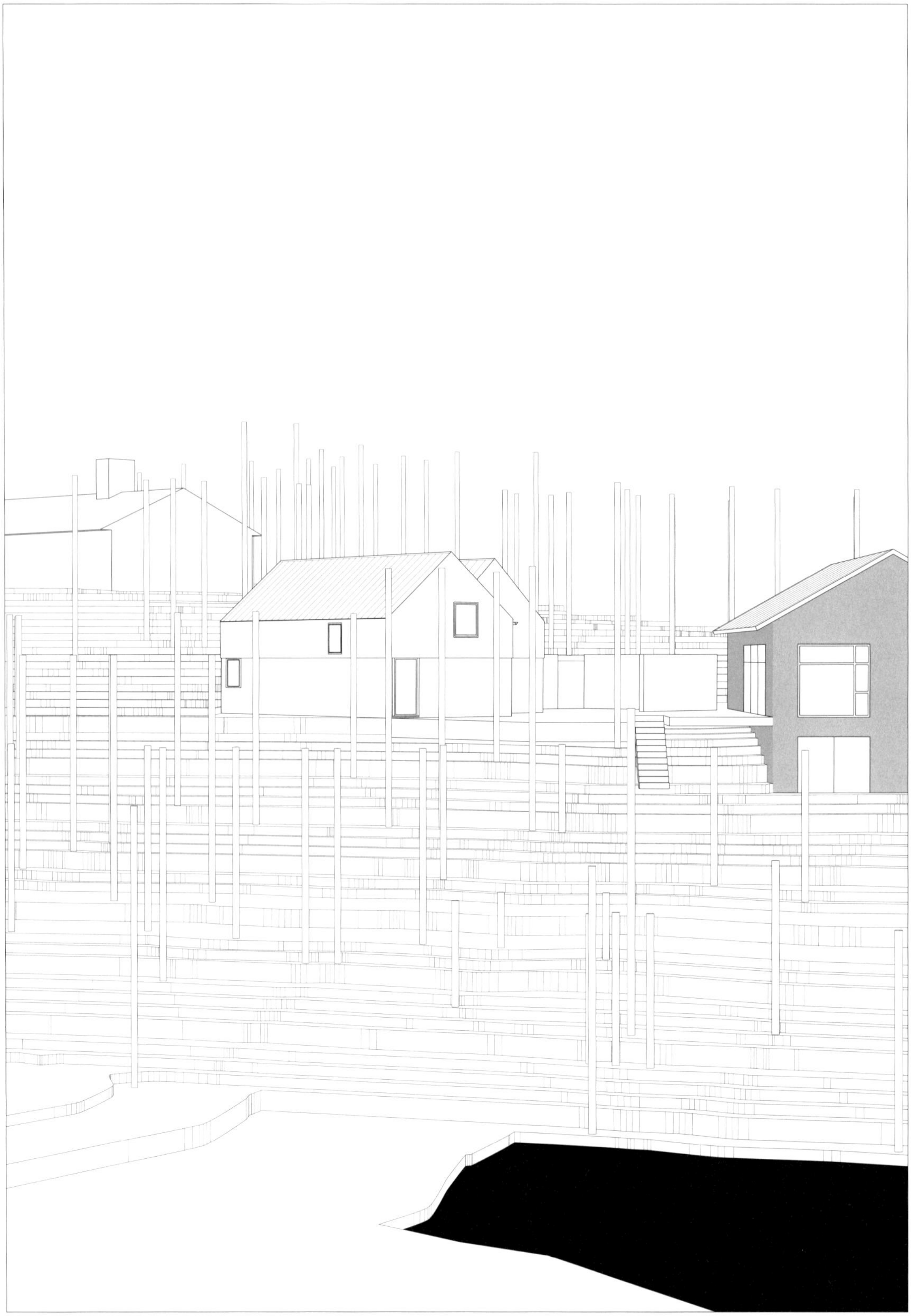

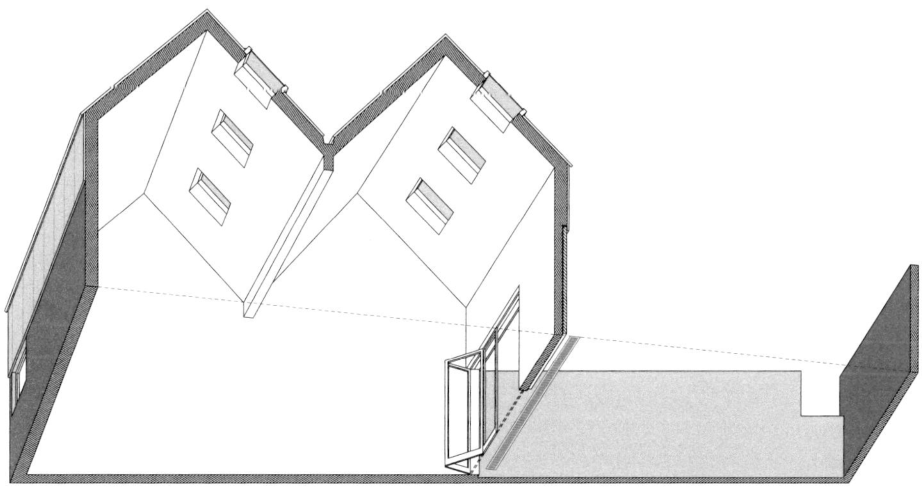

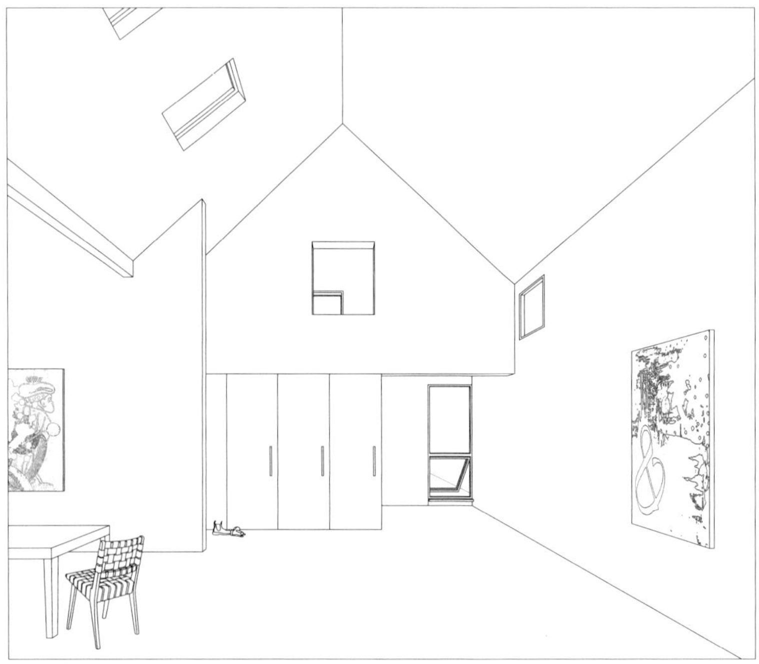

The Value of Being There

Jesús Vassallo

Charles Sheeler, *Doylestown House: Stairway, Open Door*, 1917

In 1910, the young American artist Charles Sheeler stumbled onto a small eighteenth-century farmhouse during one of his sketching expeditions in Bucks County, some twenty miles north of Philadelphia. Upon securing a lease for the house, and for the next three decades, Sheeler used the building as a second studio, retreating there for months at a time from his primary residence in the city. While it was common, almost traditional, for an artist of the period to rent or own a studio in the countryside, Sheeler's relationship to his new environment departed in fundamental ways from the picturesque tradition in which he was educated.[1]

Trained as a landscape painter, Sheeler's attention somehow turned, from the beginning of his rural retreat, towards the vernacular architecture of the area, in detriment of its rolling hills

Charles Sheeler, Bucks County Barn (with Wall), c. 1917

and lush meadows. At Bucks County, Sheeler became obsessed with his own house and the neighboring barns, a series of humble buildings which he surprisingly approached armed with a photographic camera as opposed to an easel.

At the time when Sheeler took these now famous photographs, he was under the effect of a recent trip to Paris, where an encounter with continental avant-garde art had left him concerned about the inadequacy of his training and in active search for a new approach. Sheeler's interest in the vernacular architecture of Bucks County was different from that of the Arts and Crafts movement around him: the objects and structures found in the fields of Pennsylvania were not relics of a past that needed to first be saved and then explicated, but rather desirable companions for the present, which required no explanation, but rather suggested a certain direction for the future.

This attitude was perhaps most evident in his approach towards the refurbishment of his small house, which he limited to the removal of unnecessary elements and the whitewashing of walls, choosing to keep the building without electricity or central heating. In paring down the existing construction to its bones, Sheeler did not follow an antiquarian attitude, but rather saw himself as generating a purified space and aesthetic statement, in the manner of the New York modernist art galleries that he visited and admired.[2]

At the time of his rural epiphany, Sheeler was a regular at Alfred Stieglitz's "291" gallery, famous for its groundbreaking exhibitions of both American photography and European avant-garde painting. He was also a young artist who supplemented his

Walker Evans, Houses at Edge of Delaware River, Phillipsburg, New Jersey, 1935

income through commercial architecture photography, which explains perhaps why he turned to the camera to document the buildings around him, producing in the process the body of work that would jumpstart his career.

In the context of an American art scene that struggled to find its own place in the world in the early 1900s, many artists turned to distinctly native motifs to fuel their artistic production. What is different and seminal about Sheeler, within his generation and especially in the case of his Bucks County work, is the presentness and unsentimentality of his approach to the built environment—a relationship with landscape and artifacts that is simultaneously intimate and removed.

Sheeler's images can be placed at the fountainhead of a lineage that deeply influenced the development of art and architecture in the United States throughout the twentieth century. It has been noted, for instance, how his work at Bucks County prefaced the photography of rural architecture by Walker Evans, a body of work that shares in Sheeler's luminosity and precision. In perhaps less obvious fashion, Sheeler's constant back and forth between photography and painting also prefigures the multimedia renditions of Americana by Ed Ruscha, an artist who, like Sheeler, deployed an intense but ambivalent relationship to both commercial art and its subject matter.[3]

While these are just a few specific examples, it is fair to say that a large contingent of American artists of different ilks and generations resolved the dichotomy identifying Europe as the place of high modern art and the United States as the site of a vibrant

MLTW, Sea Ranch Condominium No. 1, California, 1965

Edward Larrabee Barnes, Haystack Mountain School of Crafts, Deer Isle, Maine, 1962

and new material culture by turning their power of abstraction into their native built environment. The same proposition, however, posed more of a conflict for architects, to the extent that it reinforced the very European idea that the true North American architecture was its vernacular, leaving learned professionals in somewhat of an impossible position.

Not only did European modern architects look down on their American counterparts, they also actively exotified the country's building traditions and technologies. Think, for instance, of Le Corbusier's preference for American engineers—who he regarded as an anonymous mass—or Sibyl Moholy-Nagy's mystification of American local craftsmanship.[4] It makes sense then, that it was not until the 1960s, when the influence of the first wave of European émigrés to the United States waned, that American architects were able to revisit their vernacular modes of construction on their own terms and reconsider them as legitimate working material.

At the time, this phenomenon was perhaps best chronicled by Vincent Scully, who gathered and partially theorized a group of projects under the banner of what he defined, rather reductively, as a shingle-style revival.[5] Such wave of interest in American anonymous construction started symmetrically on both coasts around 1960, with the parallel developments of the Sea Ranch by Al Boeke and Lawrence Halprin in Sonoma County, California, and the Haystack Mountain School of Crafts by Edward Larrabee Barnes in Deer Isle, Maine.

These two projects, born out of a certain desire for immediacy and linked to the emergence of a specific type of collectivism,

Venturi and Rauch, Trubeck and Wislocki Houses, Nantucket Island, MA, 1972

Turner Brooks (with Peter Laffin and Mike Burgess, builders), Willis Higgins House, Starksboro, Vermont, 1974

MLTW, Sea Ranch Swim Club, California, 1966

were quickly followed by the very personal works of authors such as Charles Moore or Robert Venturi. Moore, who was a Sea Ranch alumn, followed a trajectory of increasing volumetric complexity throughout the decade, culminating with his Klotz House of 1971. Venturi on the other hand, seemed to gradually tame the wild impulses of his unbuilt domestic projects of the early 1960s, delivering his canonic and rather restrained Nantucket cottages in 1972.

According to Scully, whose narrative is one of style and influence, the exemplary works of Moore, Venturi, and a few others, spawned a plethora of projects across the country, just as they naturalized an approach based on the appropriation and manipulation of popular types and construction materials in highly elaborate formal compositions. Out of this group of lesser-known figures, it is perhaps the work of Turner Brooks in Vermont which better embodies the idea of an architecture that, having emerged out of a vernacular, so perfectly emulates it that it gradually recedes back into anonymity.

While interest in American vernacular construction diminished throughout the 1970s, it did not disappear completely. On the contrary, it became a fundamental formative influence for some of the most salient practitioners of the next generation. Think, for instance, of Frank Ghery's Santa Monica House of 1978, or even Steven Holl's House in Martha's Vineyard of 1988, both of which share, when considered through their constituent elements, the focus on immediacy of the previous generation of projects.[6]

To our day, such an approach that relates to anonymous architecture at a domestic scale through a mix of estrangement and earnest admiration seems to be alive and well. As a token of the

Stan Allen Architect, W/H House, Woods Hole, MA, 2018

interest of younger generations in this line of work, we could consider, for instance, how many of the *44 Low-Resolution Houses* recently gathered for an eponymous exhibition at the Princeton School of Architecture would fall comfortably under such rubric.[7]

Included in the Princeton show is Stan Allen's W/H House, a simple yet haunting project in which two volumetric primitives, ambivalent between avant-garde and vernacular resonances, are manipulated into a fragile equilibrium. In its simultaneous acceptance and distortion of the rules of light-frame construction and residential design, the house is a perfect example of an architecture that rearticulates high and low modes of production in order to interrogate its own material culture.

I would like to propose that it is precisely in its oscillation between the poles of the avant-garde and the vernacular, between the conceptual and the improvisatory, that the recent work by Stan Allen, as illustrated in the W/H House, illuminates the dynamics implied in the American lineage of projects described above, and that it does so in no small measure because of the place it occupies within the professional biography of its author.

When Stan Allen stepped down from the deanship at Princeton in 2012, few expected that his next move would be to change his permanent residence from Manhattan to the Hudson River Valley. Quite frankly, it is not uncommon for architects to use the access and visibility provided by a leadership position at a university as a springboard to an amplified and more international commercial practice, that is, to more and bigger projects in farther-away places. Allen, who at that point had a reasonably successful

Stan Allen Architect, New Maribor Art Gallery, Slovenia, 2010

office, decided instead to opt for the concentration provided by the secluded location and intimate size of projects afforded to him through his rural retreat.

The work included in this book can therefore be understood as a gradual evolution, imposed by a new context, of what was already a mature approach to practice developed through international invited competitions. At the time of his move to the Hudson River Valley, Stan Allen had recently produced his entry for the New Maribor Art Gallery in Slovenia, and was about to complete his design for the Tainan Art Museum in China. These two projects of clarified agenda and methodology are exemplary of Allen's approach to global practice, an attitude that he developed in direct conversation with colleagues such as Kazuyo Sejima or Mansilla + Tuñón, both of whom he had invited to teach in the United States in the previous decade.

With their crystalline shapes and nonhierarchical organizations, Maribor and Tainan represent Allen's own strain of internationalism, an approach where clarity of both concept and organization is valued above all, where "decisions are made at a level twice removed from material," and where a project is understood primarily as a "diagrammatic or abstract machine" capable of spawning different configurations in response to site, program, and other boundary conditions.[8]

Such emphasis on clarity is on the other hand not just ideological or based on personal preference. It relates directly to the process of natural selection that occurs within an ecosystem of design competitions where jurors from different backgrounds get

Stan Allen Architect, M/M House & Studio

Stan Allen Architect, Ghost Shed, Hudson River Valley, NY, 2017

together to review a large amount of information in a short period of time, and where the awarded architect oftentimes has to oversee the completion of the project from a different continent, many time zones away from the construction site and local partners.

That is to say that the stringency of protocol and formal organization of projects such as Maribor or Tainan is not just consistent with a modern tradition that emphasizes the internal coherence of the work. It also serves a practical purpose, to the extent that its rules and degrees of freedom allow the architect to establish a series of parameters within which to channel and control the "messy and inconsistent" reality of the global practice of architecture.[9]

Seen in the light of their predecessors, and in the arch of Allen's career, the small projects realized in the Hudson River Valley and beyond are not only part of a process of slowly shifting the focus from the large urban scale to the intimate realm of the domestic. They also tell a story of hybridizing conceptual and empirical approaches, as well as global and local logics.

In other words, the motivation to move to the Hudson River Valley was precisely to engage the work more directly, without intermediaries, and in a more continued manner. Such proximity and possibility of rapid response allowed the architect in turn to slowly devise a different set of strategies to respond to the equally messy and inconsistent conditions of a more locally grounded practice, resulting in a slow transformation of the practice itself.

The baseline to understand such process of transformation is the M/M House, and more specifically its studio addition, its sharp mineral form a direct transplant of the geometries developed for the galleries at Maribor. In this project, we witness the institutional architecture of the art museum elegantly transposed to the slightly smaller scale and less formal program of the artist studio, the directness of the translation allowed nonetheless by the affiliation of its client with the global elite of the art world.

What follows is a process in which subsequent projects are gradually informed by Allen's study of North American light-frame construction as well as his involvement with other local practices of siting and building. It is important to underscore here, however, that Allen's approach to and understanding of an American vernacular is, much like Sheeler's, unsentimental and based in equal parts on its perceived practical and aesthetic values.

Even though not explicitly one of his sources, Allen's reference to balloon-frame construction is sympathetic to Tom Peter's writing on the topic, with both authors emphasizing the industrial origin of the system, as well as its doubly democratic nature. Based on the combination of dimensional lumber and machine-cut nails, light-timber construction works with non-specialized joints, which not only makes it accessible to low-skilled labor and self-builders, but also produces structures that behave according to a statistical model, with the efforts distributed roughly evenly among its many small members and joints.[10]

Where Allen differs with Peters, and perhaps with every other commentator on the matter, is in his seeming disregard for the supposed incompatibility of such uniquely North American timber construction system with other approaches, especially to design. According to Peters, for instance, the amorphism of much light-frame suburban construction is, in fact, a symptom of a deeper divide between a European approach to architecture based on conceptual thinking, where limitation is welcome as a prerequisite for the generation of good form, and an American way of making founded on empiricism, in which limitations are systematically skewed in pursuit of personal freedom.

It is obvious by now that for Allen, who systematically works with self-imposed limitations in order to maximize his freedom as a designer, these two approaches are anything but incompatible. In that regard, the Ghost Shed and Great Plains Lyceum projects can be understood as studies in approximation, exercises where a compositional system that works with a set of a priori forms and rules is loosened through a very specific deployment of multiplicity and scale, while a construction system that is oftentimes regarded as ad hoc sees its internal rhythms reinforced in order to arrive at a resonant whole where those two metrics are rendered compatible.

While the two exhibition projects are to some extent theoretical, in the Hudson River Studio Allen was finally able to materialize

Stan Allen Architect, E/V Studio

a true synthesis of conceptual planning and pragmatic implementation, its crystalline form and precise organization rendered in the flesh of American stud-and-board construction. Built largely by the architect himself, and roughly the same size as Sheeler's small farmhouse, the compact studio is an exultant example of rural modernity, one where immediacy of construction and simplicity of way of life seem at last inextricable.

Beyond a deepening knowledge of a certain scale of work and type of construction, working in the Hudson River Valley has also

Stan Allen Architect, Peter Saul Studio

enabled Allen's practice to evolve in other ways, and it has done so, I would argue, through a relative lowering of stakes. Through its everyday engagement with building, a local practice of finer granularity is conducive to smaller jobs—some for the architect himself, others for acquaintances—small commissions not meant for publication that allow the architect in turn to lower the guard and work at a more subconscious level.

Out of these supposedly minor projects, which include various outbuildings and sheds, the most remarkable is the studio that Allen designed for the painter Peter Saul. Peter and his wife Sally, a ceramic artist, had been working from a small garage in the back of their property, but had outgrown the tiny building and needed more space. Limited by a small budget and other site constraints, the only reasonable solution became to build a two-story volume on the existing foundation.

Faced with a minimal budget that mandated a hardcore no-frills approach, and unable to control the footprint or even orientation of the building, the role of the architect was reduced here to enacting corrections on a volume dictated by external constraints. These small volumetric adjustments were then complemented by the design of the cladding—in an oversized, undulating pattern—resulting in an unstable and uncanny building that manages to exude complexity in spite of its austerity and straightforwardness.

With the Peter Saul Studio Allen enters a reactive mode of production, even welcoming modifications during construction, in a remarkable development for an architect who historically front-loads each project through the design of the design process itself.

Stan Allen Architect, J/S House

Stan Allen Architect, J/S House

A similarly reactive approach is found in other works of relatively larger scope, such as the J/S House, an extension project where Allen works to offset an idiosyncratic late-1980s home with the addition of a volume of similar size and proportion.

While the project for the J/S House was jumpstarted by rehearsing a series of roof geometries reminiscent of his Sagaponak House, Allen soon realized that the speaking architecture of the original building required a muter partner, focusing for the remainder of the design process on a careful consideration of proportion. Though restrained, the new metal cube responds assertively to the existing building, establishing a dialogue between its oversized punched openings and the reduced bays of the trabeated ground floor in the original house. Remarkable in person, the result is a building that does not whitewash the awkwardness of the preexisting building, yet manages to dignify its small monumentality.

As Allen becomes more comfortable in his new setting, more fluent in the language of construction, and more confident in his capacity to extract expression out of seemingly small moves in small buildings, the projects in turn grow more exploratory. A good example of this is the K/S Library, where the same form-making protocols used in the Hudson River Studio produce a looser massing and higher degree of spatial complexity, features shared by other ongoing projects.

It is indeed exciting to think of this series of buildings as a beginning, and to anticipate what directions the work may take as the network becomes denser across the valley and new types and scales come into play. Seen in that light, as a collective of semi-anonymous buildings scattered in the landscape—the way Allen likes to think of them—these projects also point towards the idea of a rural contemporary architecture and highlight the importance of architects engaging the country.

To acknowledge that the Hudson River Valley, with its concentration of art and architecture, is not an average rural county does not diminish the merit of an architecture that has found a way to be urbane and non-condescending in its rural condition. Just as Sheeler developed a precise image of America's rapidly industrializing landscape, Allen's body of work presents us with a positive vision for its postindustrial future, an unromantic acknowledgment and acceptance of the gradient between urban and rural conditions in all of its complexity and opportunity.

It is precisely in this relationship to context that the photography of Scott Benedict, which illustrates this book, becomes the perfect companion and window into Allen's work. A local, Benedict is free to visit Allen's projects repeatedly, almost casually, in an echo of the architect's constant comings and goings between studio and construction site. Being present allows Benedict not only to portray the sites in different light conditions or different in such a way seasons, but most importantly, to gain a degree of familiarity with the buildings that renders them deeply enmeshed in everyday life.

Most fittingly, Benedict's photography brings to the foreground some of the tension between abstraction and realism present in Allen's work as identified in this text. On the one hand, his use of black-and-white photography emphasizes the sharp forms and exacting geometries of Allen's volumes, bringing to mind the

Stan Allen Architect,
E/V House & Studio

canonic images of modernist architecture taken by Ezra Stoller or Hendrich Blessing. On the other hand, with his very personal and intuitive approach to framing, which is closer to documentary photography, Benedict refuses to reify or aggrandize the small buildings, concentrating instead on narrating their lives and the passage of time. It is thus perhaps through Benedict's visual diary that we best understand the architect's motivation in moving to the country, as we witness the dissolution of the boundary between building and living, between artistic production and its enjoyment as part of everyday life, and grasp the value of actually being there.

Stan Allen Architect, E/V House & Studio

1. Karen Lucic, *Sheeler in Doylestown* (Allentown: Allentown Art Museum, 1997), 17.

2. Ibid., 19.

3. This debt is most obvious in Ruscha's large-format crayon renditions of apartment buildings based on his photographs of Los Angeles, which eerily recall Sheeler's painstakingly precise drawings of his farmhouse performed with the same technique. In both cases, drawing augments the degree of abstraction previously achieved with photography to put forward a further aestheticized if also more desolate image of the everyday.

4. I am thinking here of Le Corbusier's famous diatribe in *Toward an Architecture*: "Let us listen to the counsels of American engineers. But let us beware of American architects." Also of Sibyl Moholy-Nagy's musings about a North American spirit of craft in her *Native Genius in Anonymous Architecture* (New York: Horizon, 1957).

5. Vincent Scully, *The Shingle Style Today, or the Historian's Revenge* (New York: George Braziller, 1974).

6. In the case of Steven Holl, this interest started years earlier through a series of publications on American housing typologies. See, for instance, Steven Holl, "Rural and Urban House Types," in *Pamphlet Architecture* 9 (1983): 5–27.

7. Michael Meredith, *44 Low-Resolution Houses* (Princeton: Princeton SoA, 2018).

8. The latter is a quote from Deleuze and Guattari's *A Thousand Plateaus* that Allen uses to illustrate an emphasis on performance in his early writing. For more on the Tainan and Maribor projects and their relationship to Allen's thinking, see Benjamin Wilke, ed., *Stan Allen: Four Projects* (Columbus: Knowlton School of Architecture, 2017).

9. See Stan Allen, "Introduction: Practice vs. Project," in *Practice: Architecture, Technique and Representation* (New York: G+B Arts International, 2000), xii.

10. Tom F. Peters, "An American Culture of Construction," in *Perspecta* vol. 25 (1989): 142–61.

MA

HISTO

TE
RIAL

RIES

"The balloon-frame building with its skeleton of thin machine-cut studs and covering of clapboards grew out of the seventeenth-century farmhouses of the early settlers [. . .] The balloon frame has kept its vitality for a whole century and is still used extensively. This simple and efficient construction is thoroughly adapted to the requirements of contemporary architects."

Sigfried Giedion

The Balloon Frame Revisited

Balloon frame construction, Omaha Reservation, Nebraska, 1877

The balloon frame is an emblematic American invention: collective, anonymous, and makeshift. As settlers moved west, they needed a way to build quickly and cheaply, working with readily available materials. Wood was plentiful, and sawmills easily erected. Balloon framing took advantage of two nineteenth-century innovations: precut dimensional lumber and mass-produced nails. Unlike the heavy timber frames associated with European and early American construction (which required skilled mortise and tenon joinery), these lightweight standardized elements allowed relatively unskilled builders to build rapidly and cheaply. “The balloon frame,” writes Giedion, “marks the point at which industrialization began to penetrate housing.”

Logging in Wisconsin, c. 1910

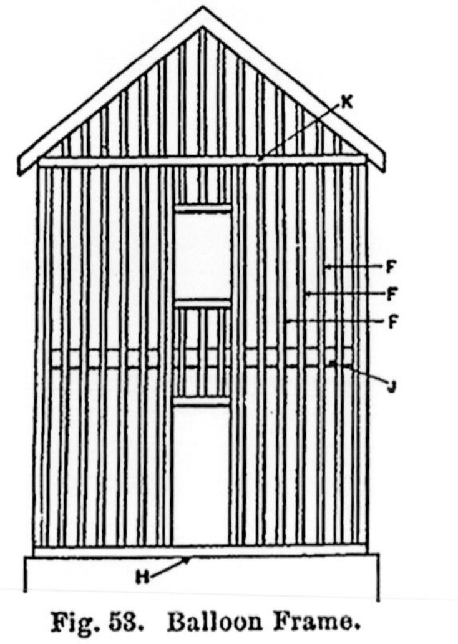

Diagram of balloon framing

House moving, Great Plains, c. 1915

Stanley Tigerman, Black Barn, Frog Hollow, Berrien Springs, Michigan, USA, 1973–1974

The industrialization of building, in turn, triggered a demand for wood. Over the course of the nineteenth century, Chicago became the nexus of an emerging lumber industry, with raw materials—white pine from the Michigan and Wisconsin forests—shipped inexpensively by water to the city for processing. The balloon frame accelerated the opening of the western plains, as materials could be shipped by rail, with simple houses and barns built on site by local laborers. Although the Great Fire of 1871 discouraged the use of wood-frame construction in the city, Chicago remained the largest supplier of dimensional lumber in the country until the end of the century, when Midwestern forest stocks were finally depleted.

In his seminal book, *Nature's Metropolis: Chicago and the Great West*, William Cronon documents how the development of Chicago was intricately tied to its larger ecological region. The city's three primary industries—grain trading, meatpacking, and lumber—were each connected to a network of regional ecologies, and the expansion of these industries had devastating consequences for both the tallgrass prairies and the northern forests. What Cronon's environmental history teaches us is that materials do not exist in a vacuum, and that the city, architecture, and the region are all interconnected. A rethinking of balloon-frame construction in the present is a rethinking of architecture's history through material, ecology, and building technique.

Lightweight dimensional lumber is still the preferred technique for small-scale construction in the United States. Engineered lumber now allows greater spans, and platform construction has superseded true balloon-frame construction, but the essential architectural characteristics of the technique—a screen-like wall that acts as a lightweight, permeable membrane—persist. Vincent Scully has identified the taut envelope effect of the balloon frame, which emphasizes surface over structure, as a particularly American way of building. Like the Jeffersonian grid, it is standardized and democratic yet allows individual expression. It works in series, arraying many small parts so that no single element or connection is crucial. It is, above all, pragmatic, tied into networks of supply and distribution, and readily available tools and techniques.

Stan Allen Architect, Ghost Shed

1. GHOST SHED: COPY/PASTE/TRIM

Originally developed as an exhibition installed at the School of Architecture at New York Institute of Technology in Old Westbury, Long Island this was the first of three projects to explore the architectural potentials of balloon-frame construction. The title refers to operations in computer modeling utilized to determine the form of the object constructed in the gallery.

The project originated with a client commission for a series of speculative houses for a rural site in upstate New York. The brief was to respect the local vernacular, and to work with a recognizable house form. But we didn't want to remain at the level of sentimental recall, or to create a complicated assemblage. Our strategy was to multiply, intersect, and trim these simple elements, to create a set of variations that would each be unique, yet related to each other and would recall the iconic form of a pitch-roofed house. The basic geometry and the logic of aggregation disappear into a new whole. Parts are familiar, but their repetition produces unexpected effects.

The exhibition was an opportunity to realize one of these unbuilt variations. The construction exhibited in the gallery was an uncanny object, too big to be a model but too small to be a house—a 1:4 version of the earlier design. The insistent verticals of the wood scaffolding recall balloon-frame construction, while the translucent skin creates a lantern-like effect, revealing the presence of the support behind. This compound volume is intended to recall the memory of the house while triggering other associations beyond the domestic.

When the exhibition closed, the project was reinstalled in an open field in the Hudson River Valley. There is a double displacement at work here: the shed floats above the ground, revealing the wood frame—a ghostly object not quite fixed in place—while the changing effects of reflection and transparency create an ambivalence of surface and support, interior and exterior. Although not inhabitable, the scale and character of this "object in a field" acquire a social dimension when placed in the public realm.

Stan Allen Architect, W/H House

2. W/H HOUSE

This unbuilt proposal—a live/work residence for an artist on a wooded site on Cape Cod—continues the investigation of the expressive potential of the taut building envelope implied by balloon-frame construction. In his *The Shingle Style Today*, Vincent Scully underscored the affinity between the New England vernacular and the Shingle Style of the late nineteenth century. Both treated the building skin as a taut membrane, stretched over a wood skeleton, and expressed as volume over mass. This project works consciously in that tradition, while introducing a more disciplined geometry, and serial repetition.

The lot is small and the adjoining houses close by. Duplicating a faceted volume generated from the five-sided plan articulates indoor and outdoor common spaces, and orients bedroom windows away from adjacent structures. The repetition and aggregation of these compact elements create a hybrid object: at once two identifiable bodies and an integrated whole. The project has an unforced complexity appropriate to the constraints of site and program.

The volumes are compact and clean, with overhangs minimized and openings deliberately placed in response to views and movement. There is a certain informality in the window placement, dictated by the needs of the interior. In profile, there is a constant play of familiarity and surprise as the viewer encounters variations of the pitched-roof geometry produced by the intersection of a regular profile with a complex plan figure.

Stan Allen Architect, Lyceum, exhibition proposal

3. LYCEUM

Exhibited at the 2017 Chicago Biennial, *Make New History*, curated by Sharon Johnston and Mark Lee, this project addresses architecture's material history as an expanded field of possible balloon-frame constructions. For the Biennial, we proposed a hypothetical design of a public institution that explored aggregation, part-to-whole relationships, repetition, and field-like strategies.

Growing out of the mechanics' institutes of the early nineteenth century, the American Lyceum movement was an early form of progressive, community-based education. *Lyceum* refers to the temple in Ancient Greece where public philosophical debates took place. Originating in the Northeast, and later spreading to the Midwest, the Lyceum Movement flourished in the years before and after the Civil War as voluntary local associations that gave citizens an opportunity to hear lectures and debates on topics of current interest. Ralph Waldo Emerson, Frederick Douglass, Henry David Thoreau, Nathaniel Hawthorne, and Susan B. Anthony all lectured frequently. The Lyceum Movement is credited with the improvement of schools and the development of local libraries and museums in the United States.

The part-to-whole aggregation of the architectural proposal mirrors the democratic aspirations of the Lyceum Movement: an assembly of individual elements that fuse into a larger whole while retaining the identity of each part. For this project, we propose to revive the spirit of the Lyceum with local schools and community-based places of debate and exchange. The model exhibited and developed in plan is a flexible prototype; the number and orientation of the parts can change, while the material expression, the iconic profile, and unique identity will persist over a number of possible variations.

> *"In the Old World the nuances and differences between nations form the main focus of the picture. In the New World, man and his productions disappear, so to speak, in the midst of a wild and outsize nature."*[1]

All three of these hypothetical projects work with episodes in the history of an ongoing dialogue between landscape and the American imagination. The presence of this vast territory is deeply embedded in the American consciousness. Nature has a different presence in the Americas: larger, wilder, and more complex. The Americas are a young geology, still in formation, and all this feeds the notion of possibility and self-invention. The balloon frame is intimately tied to this history; it links together logging practices in the Midwest, New England vernacular building, and the settlement of the Great Plains. It is simultaneously material, ecological, and cultural. Places are more than just geography; they are constructed in the imagination and deeply embedded in complex material histories.

1. Alexander von Humboldt, *Personal Narrative of a Journey to the Equinoctial Regions of the New Continent*, London: Penguin, 1995 (1807).

GHOST SHED

2017

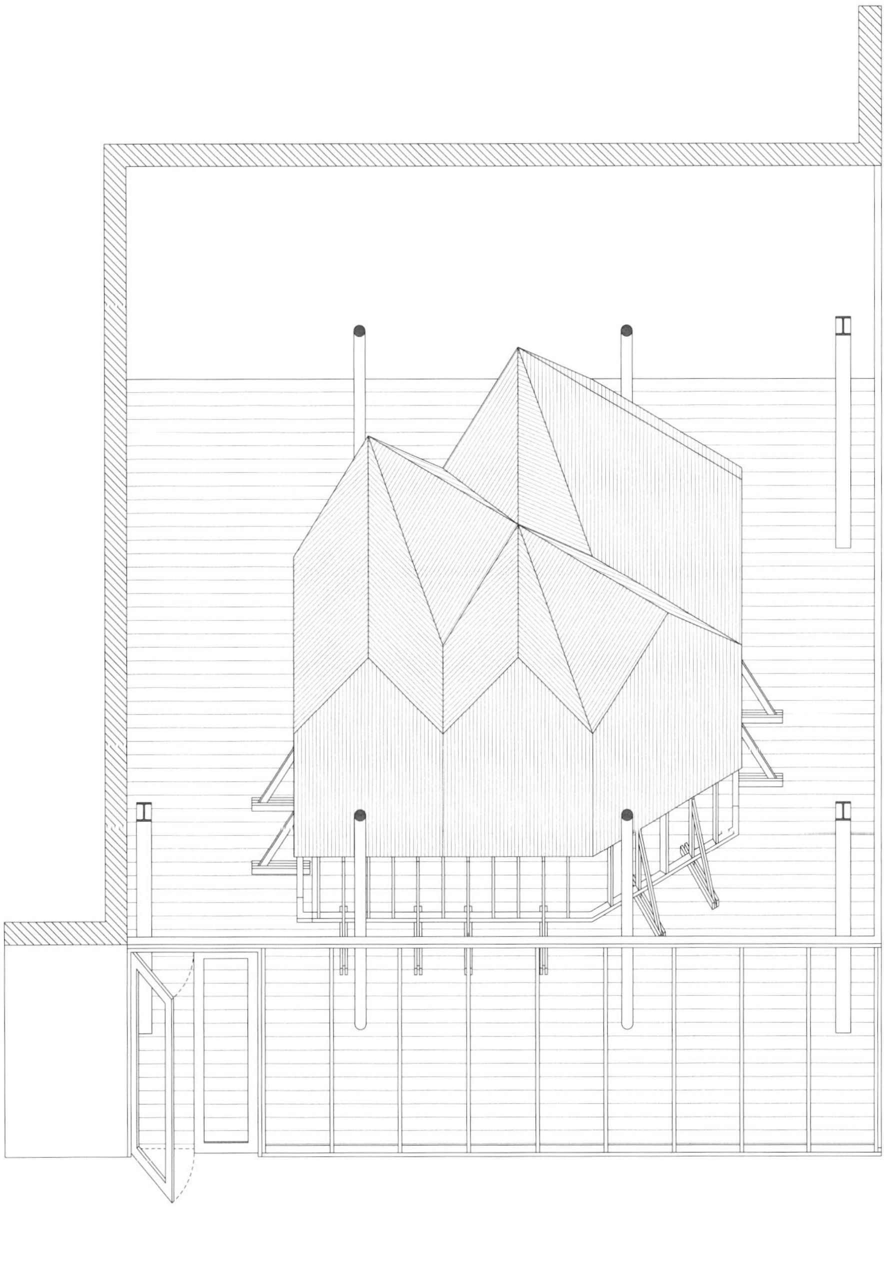

Long Island/
Hudson River Valley, NY

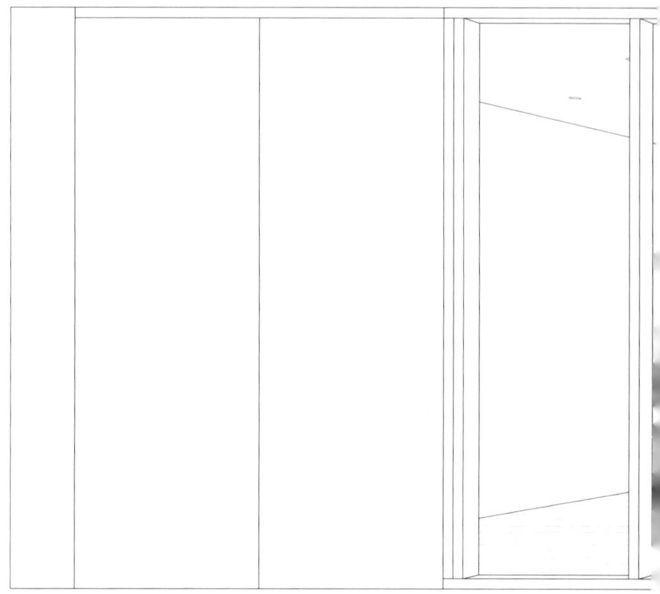

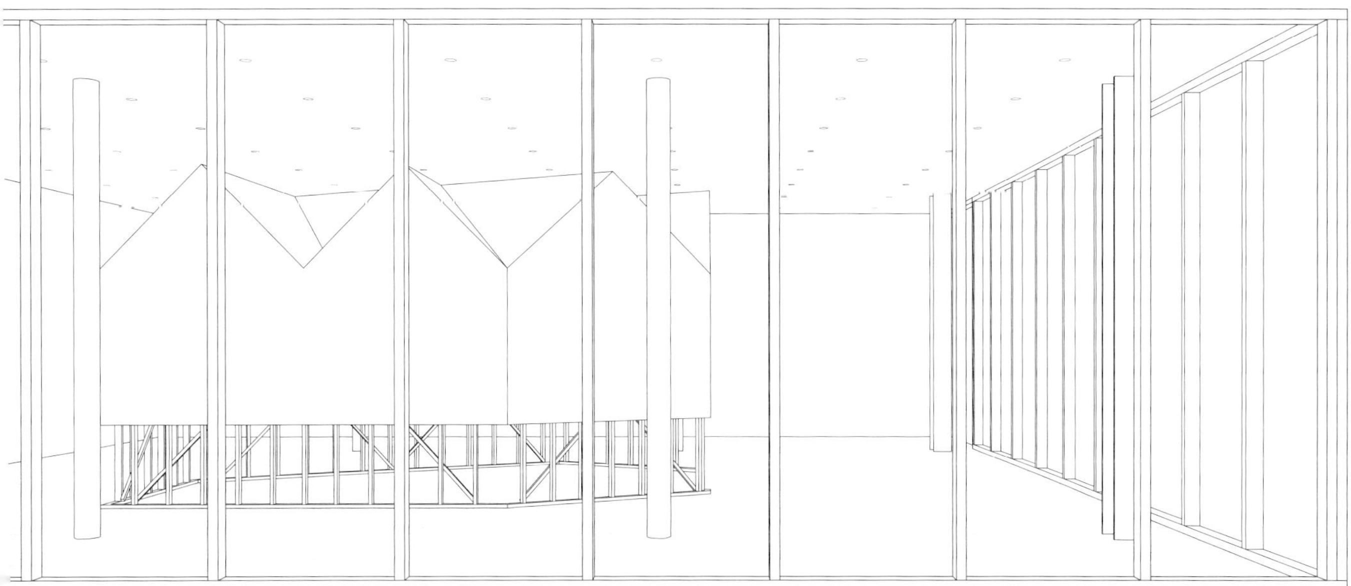

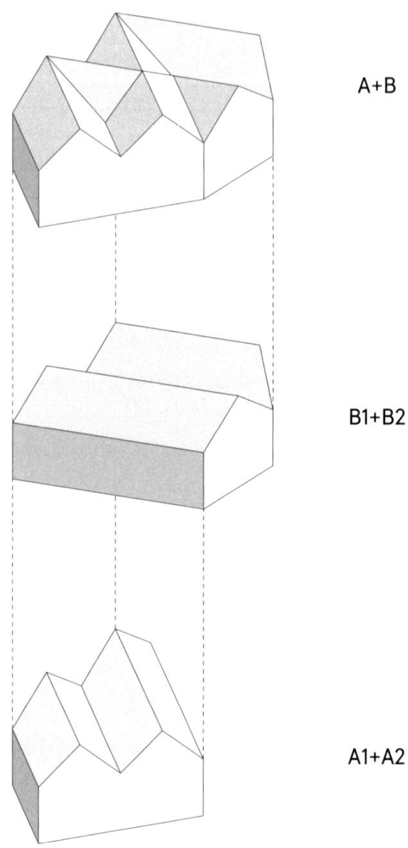
A+B
B1+B2
A1+A2

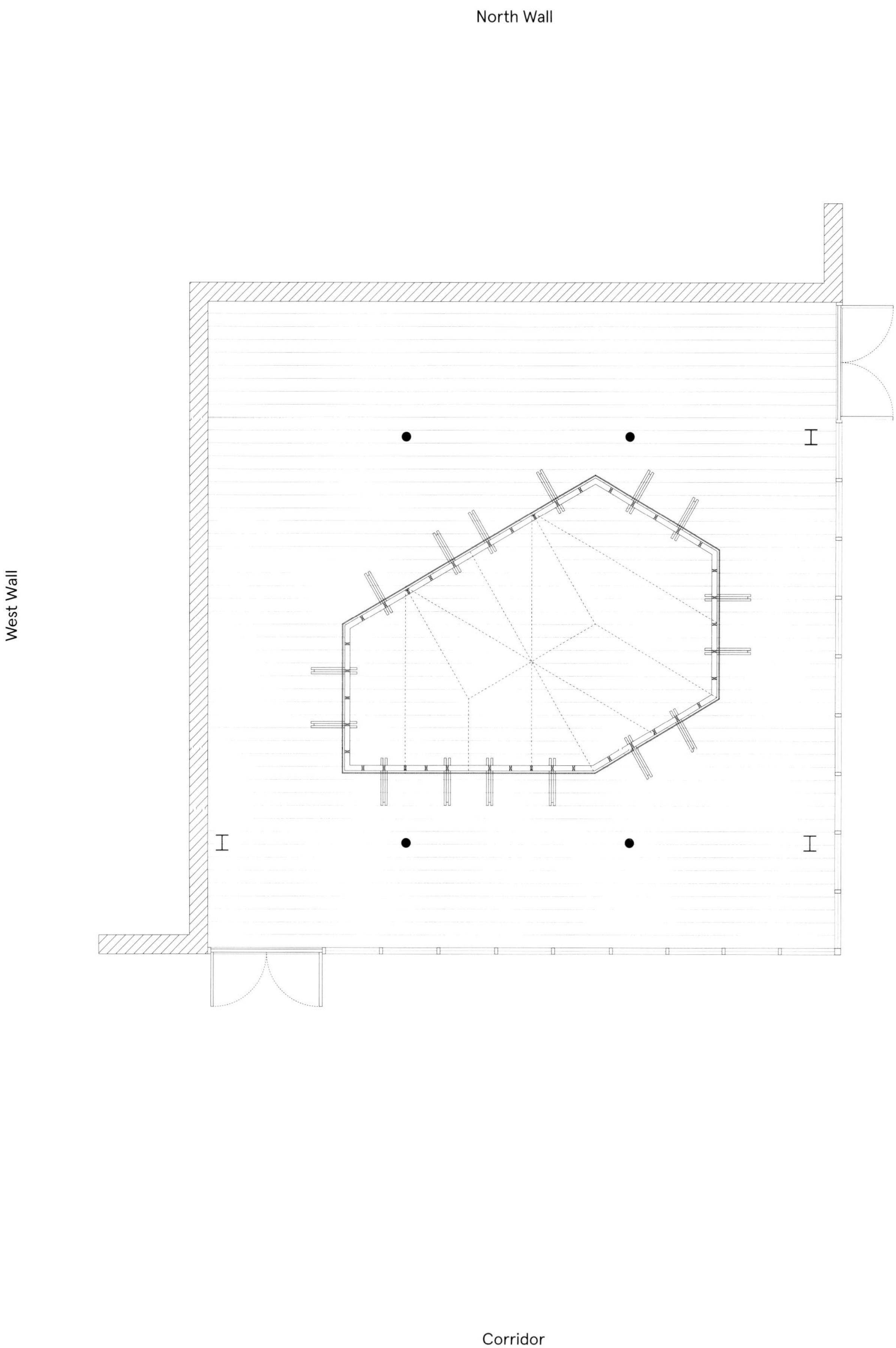

North Wall
West Wall
Corridor

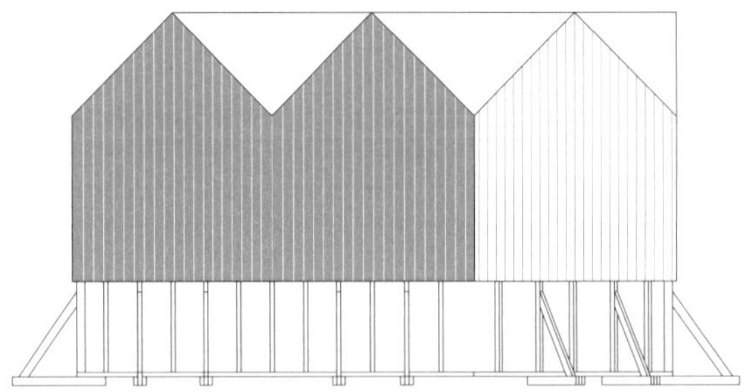

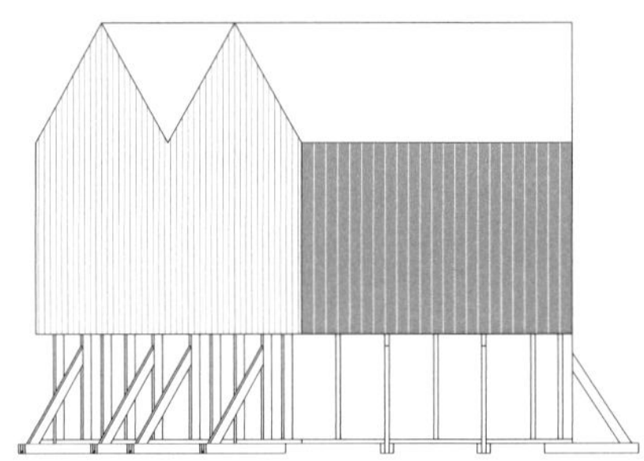

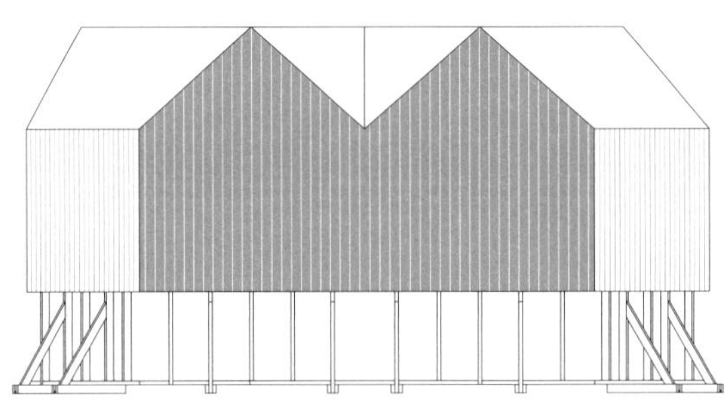

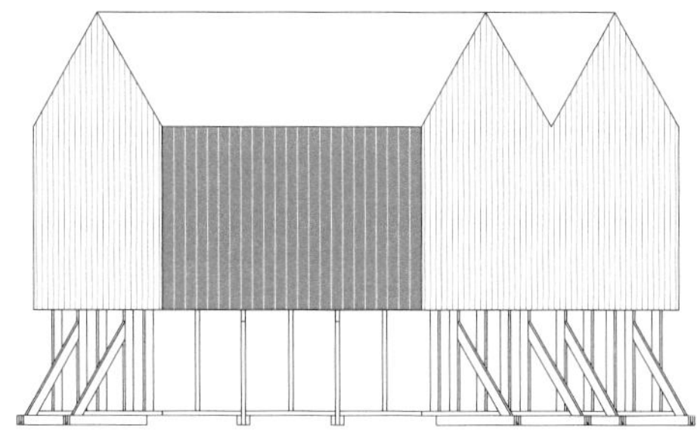

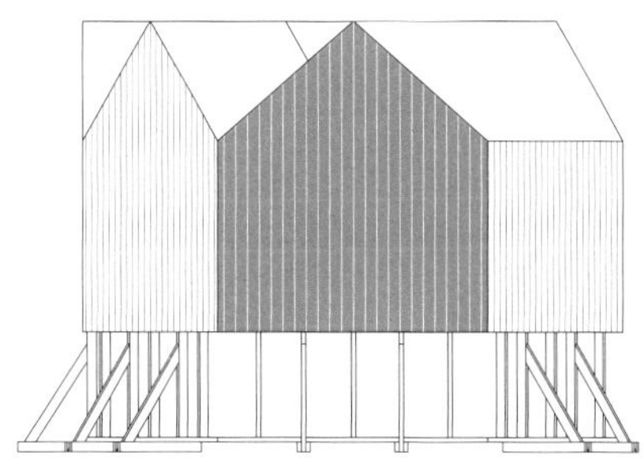

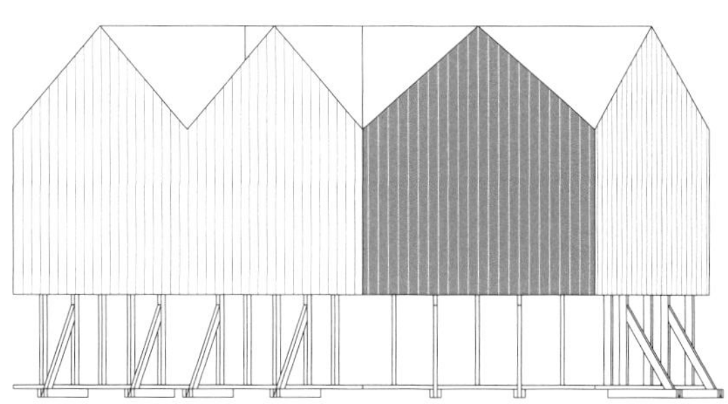

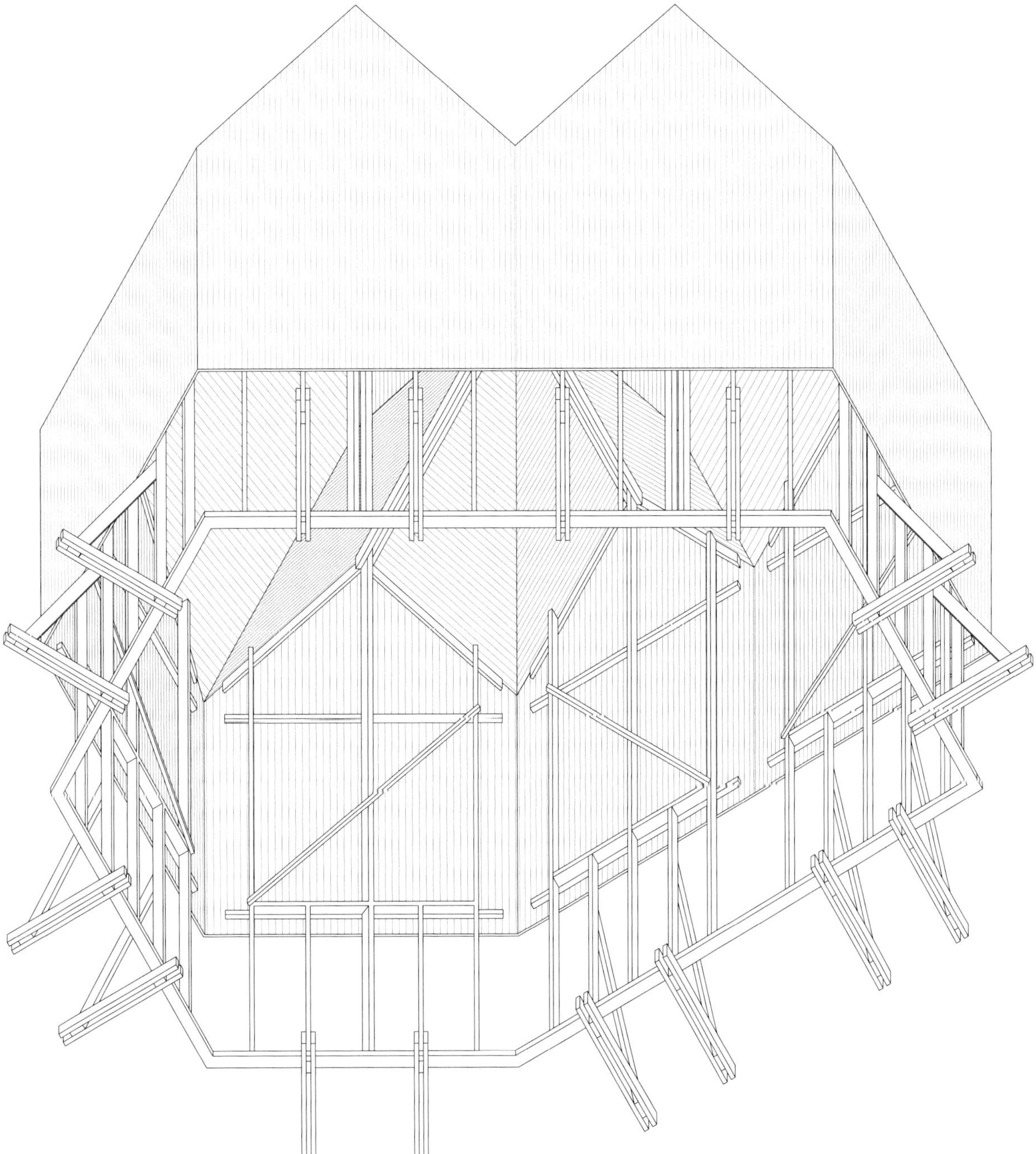

W/H HOUSE

2018

Woods Hole, MA

CB FND
N 74°36'00" W
206.72'
S 03°46'00" W
75.00'
136.69'
S 79°59'10" E
S 38°53'10" E
100.00'
EDGE OF PAVEMENT
EDGE OF GRAVEL
EDGE OF CURB
CURB
WATER METER
REC 504
OHW
SETBACK

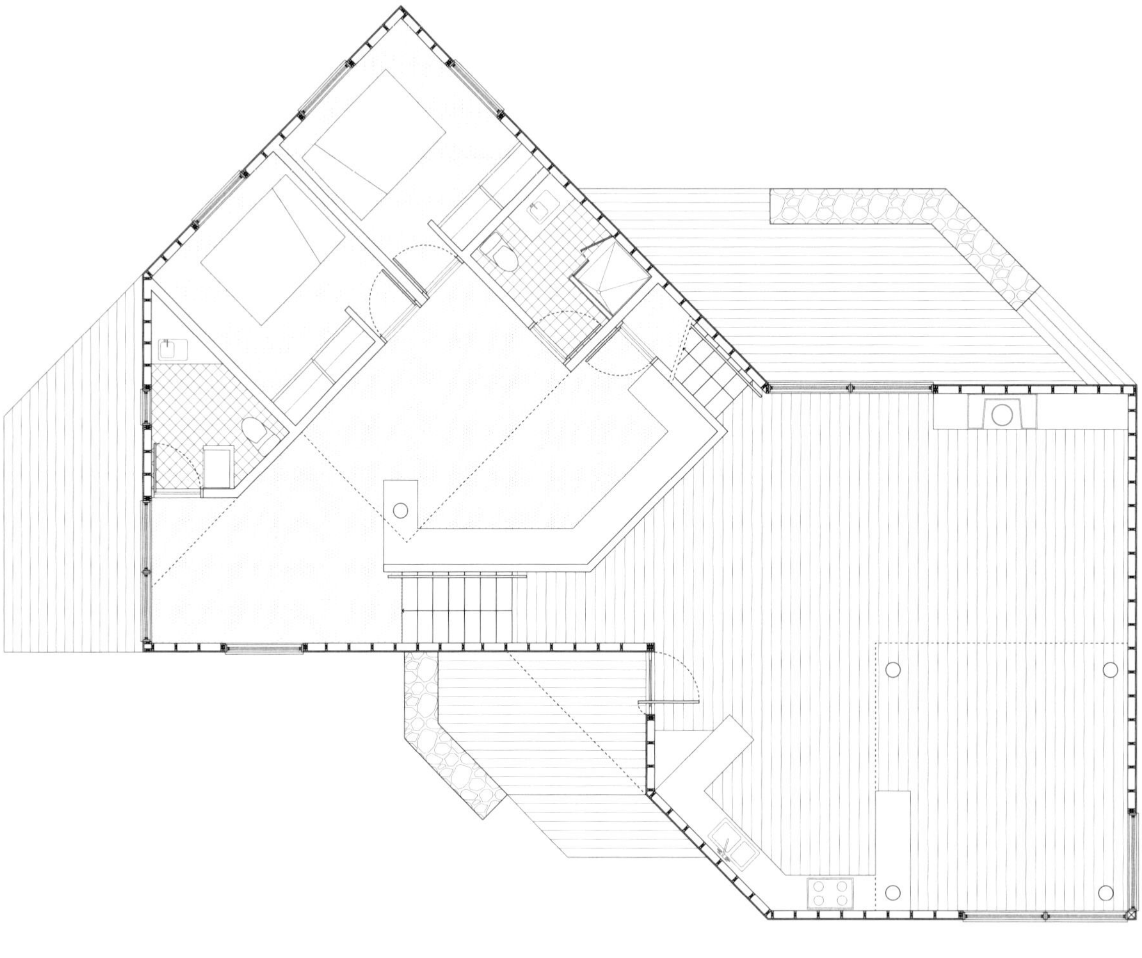

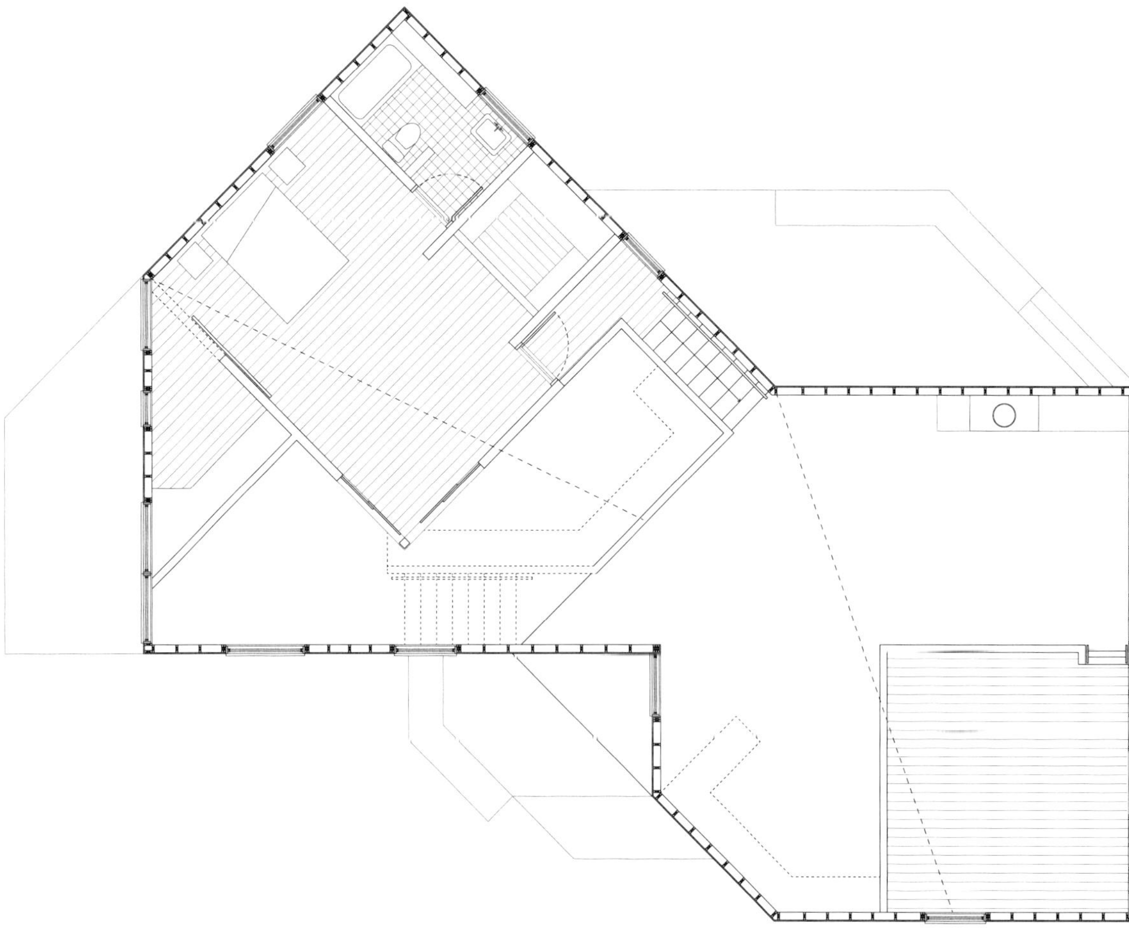

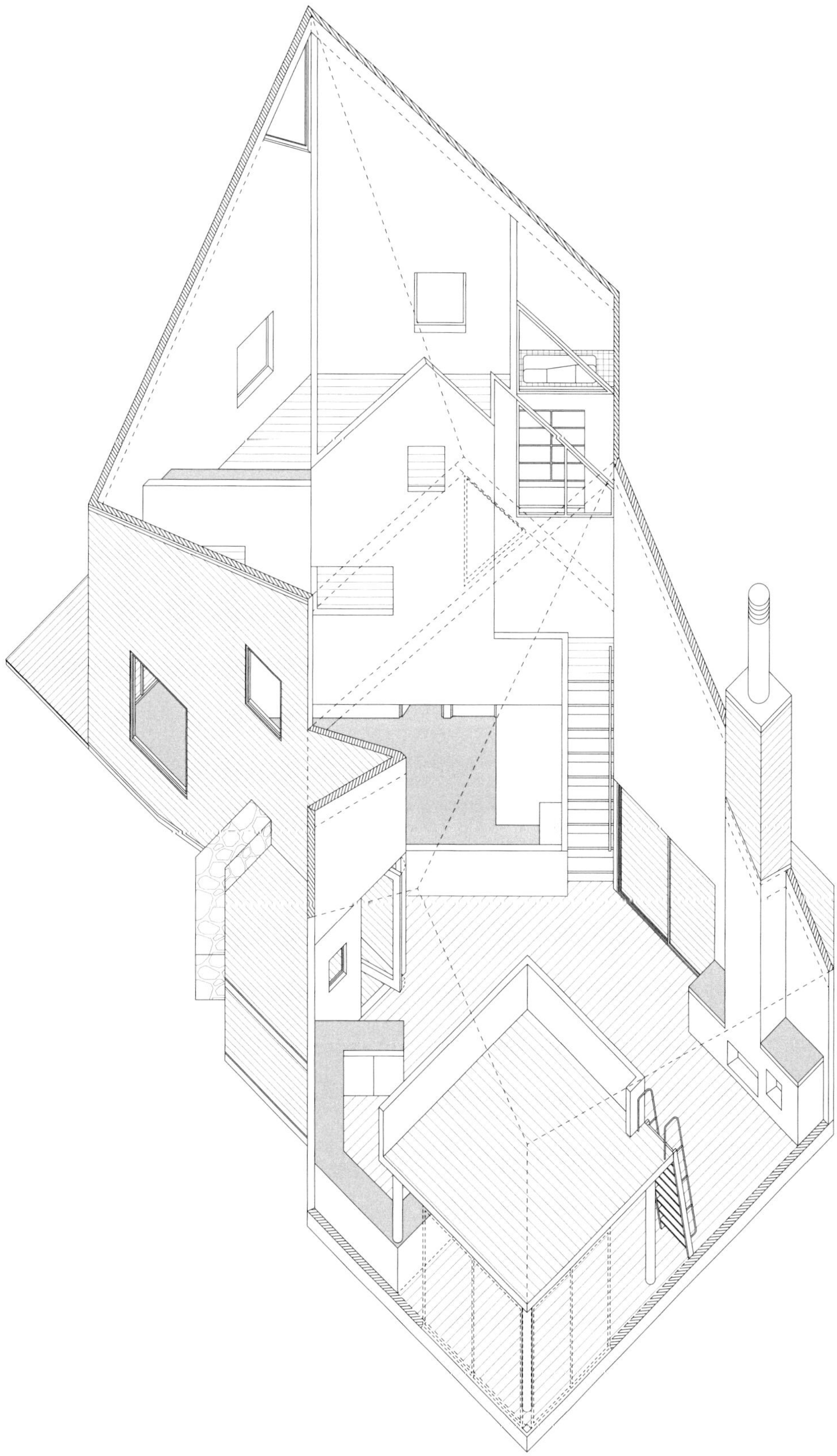

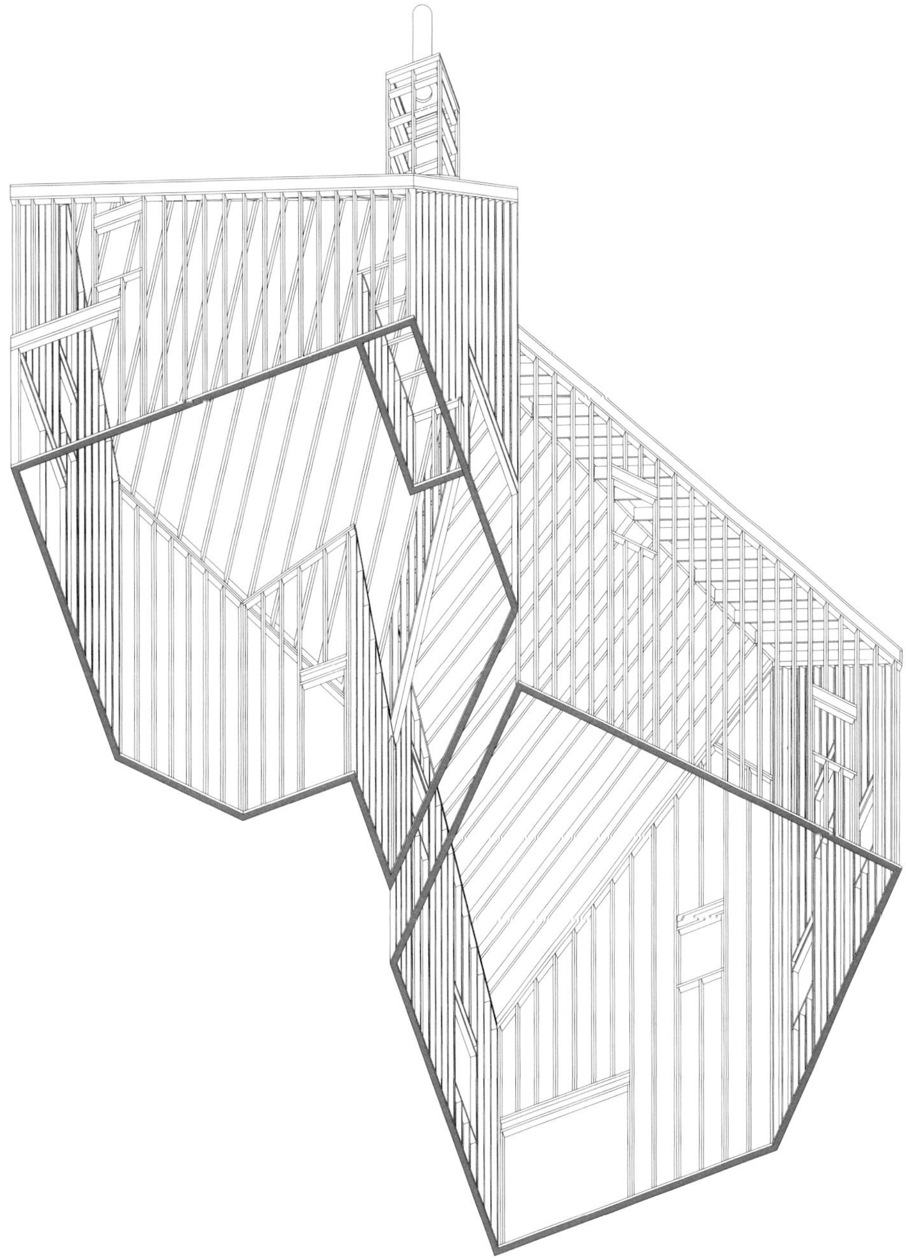

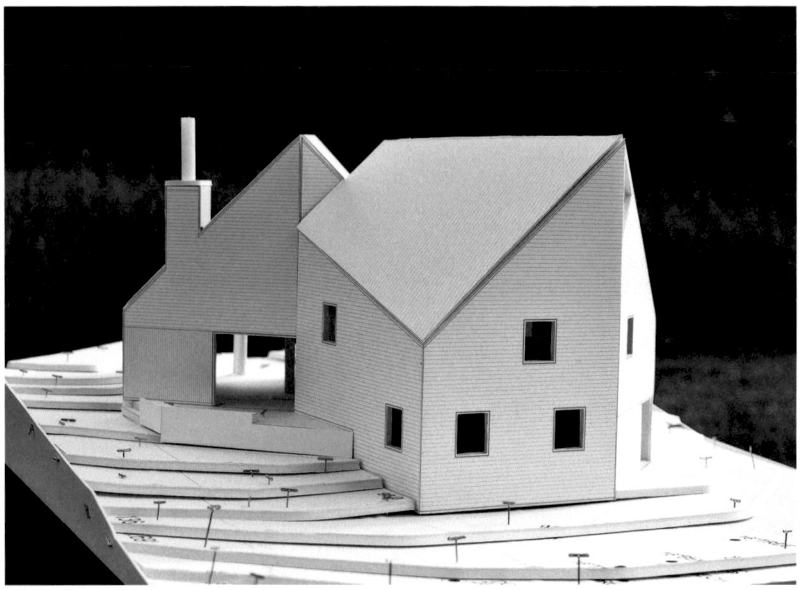

LYCEUM

2017

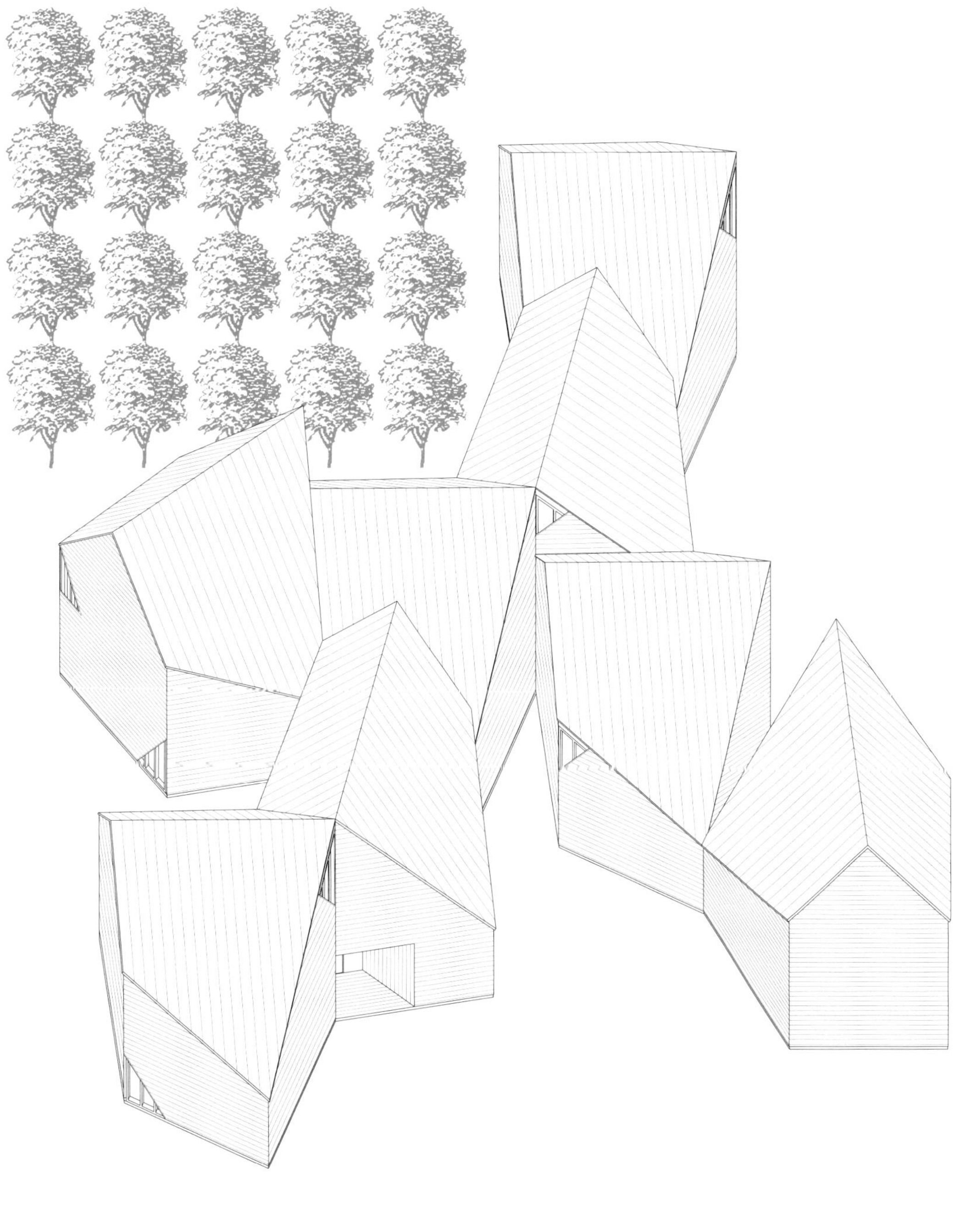

Chicago Biennial, Chicago, IL

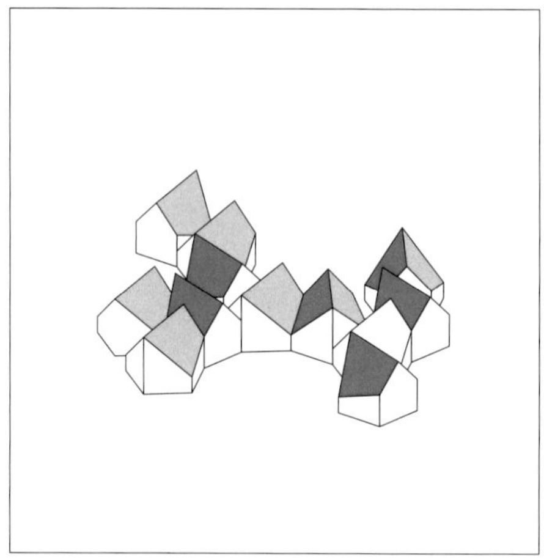

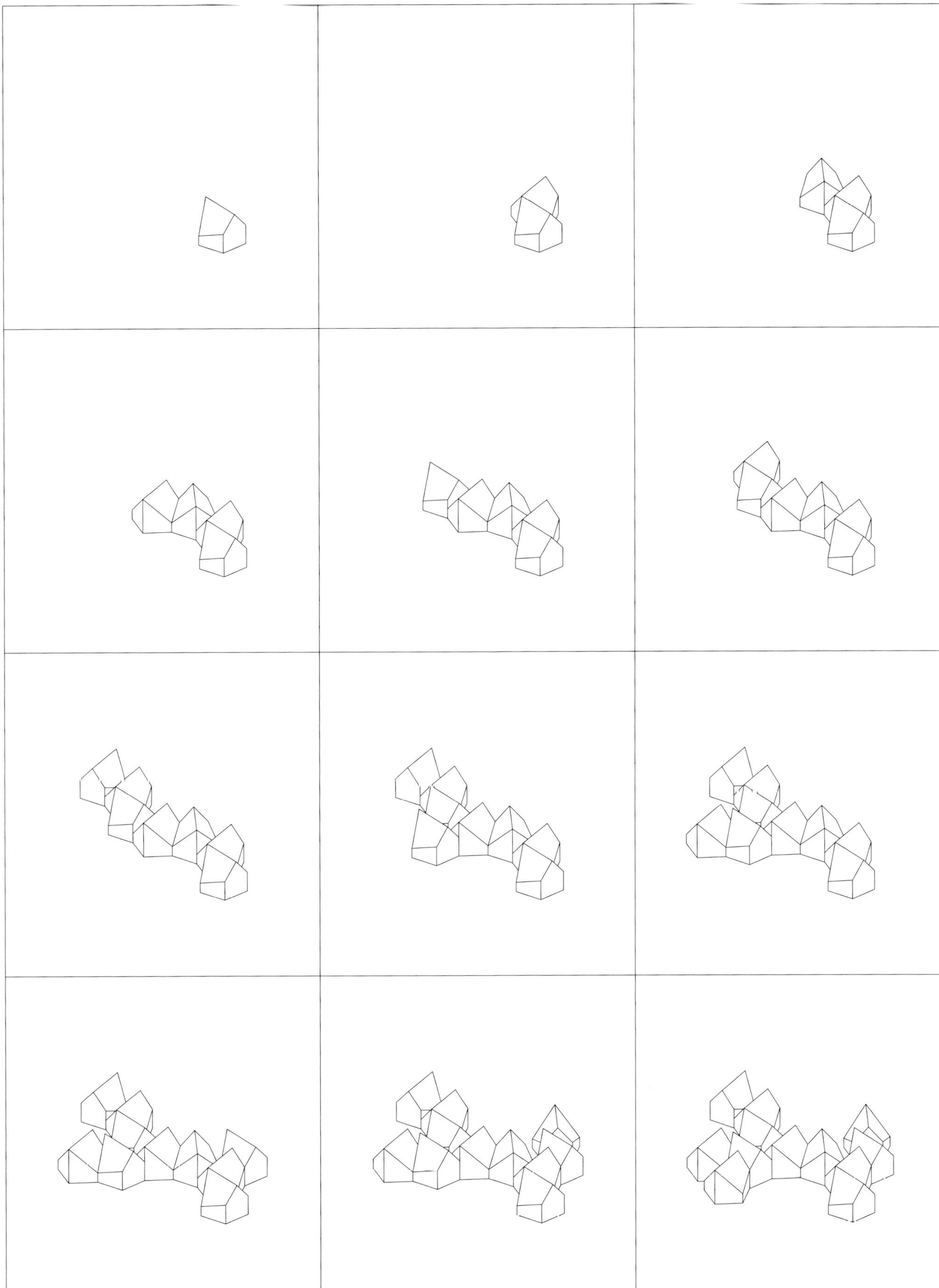

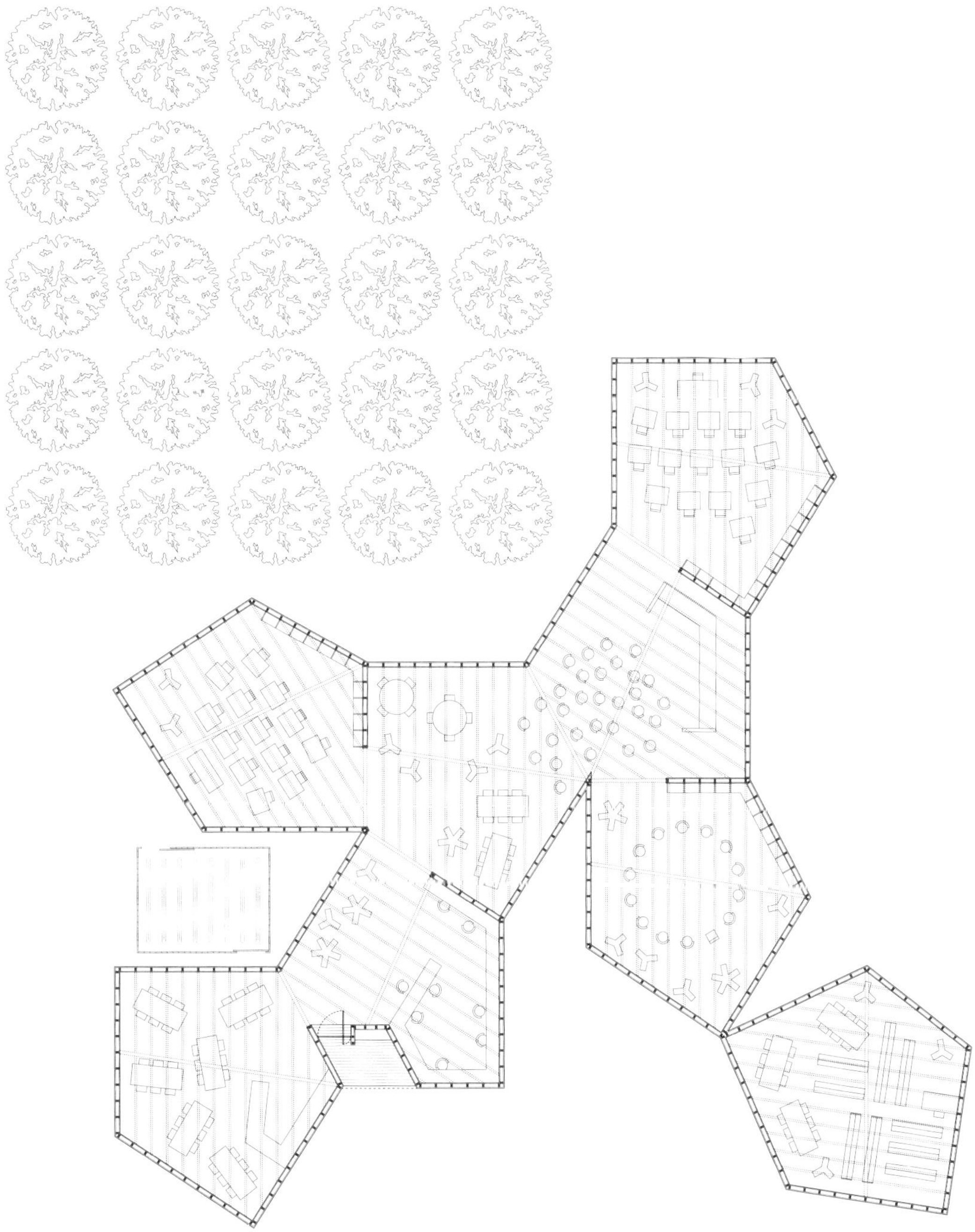

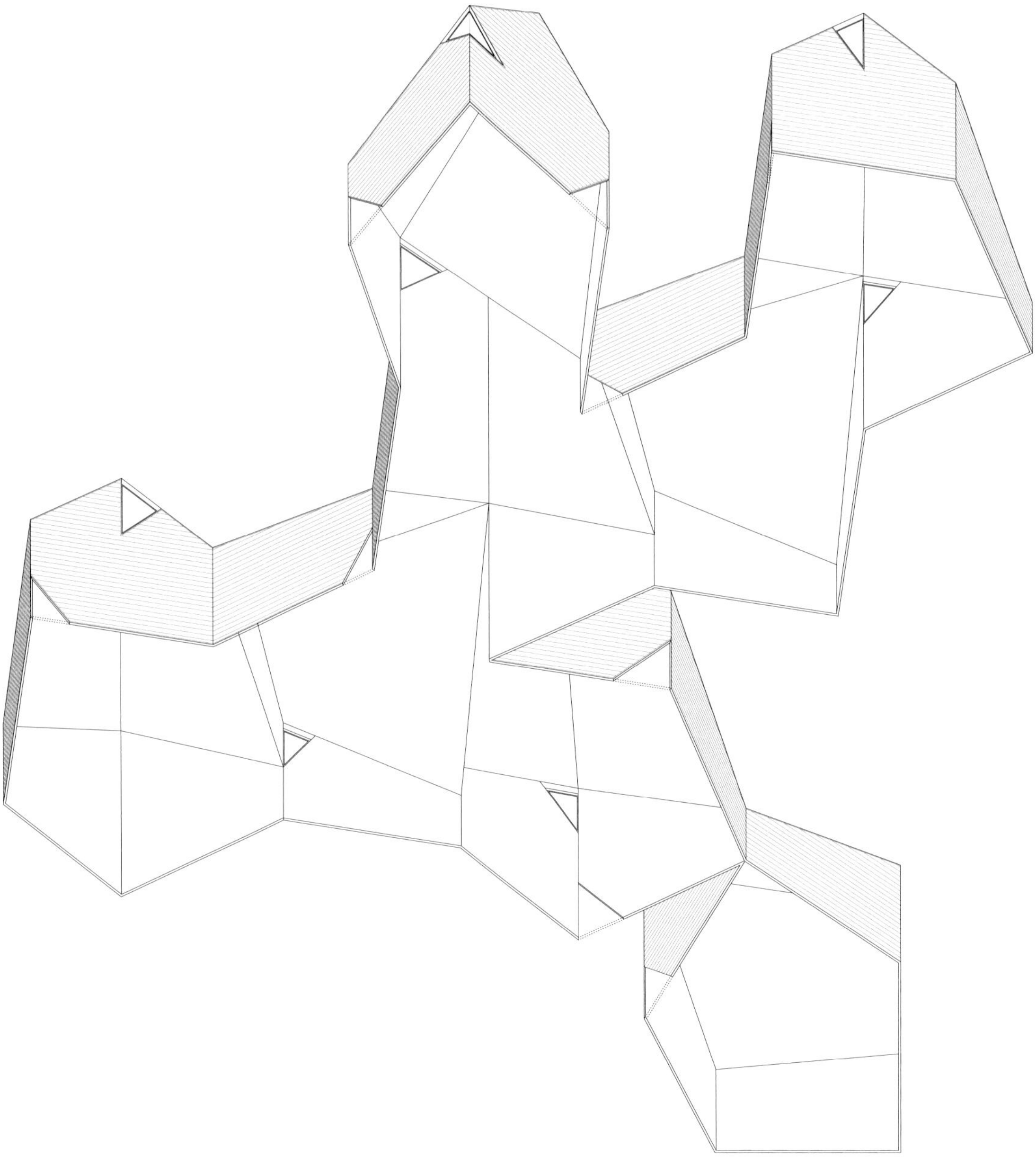

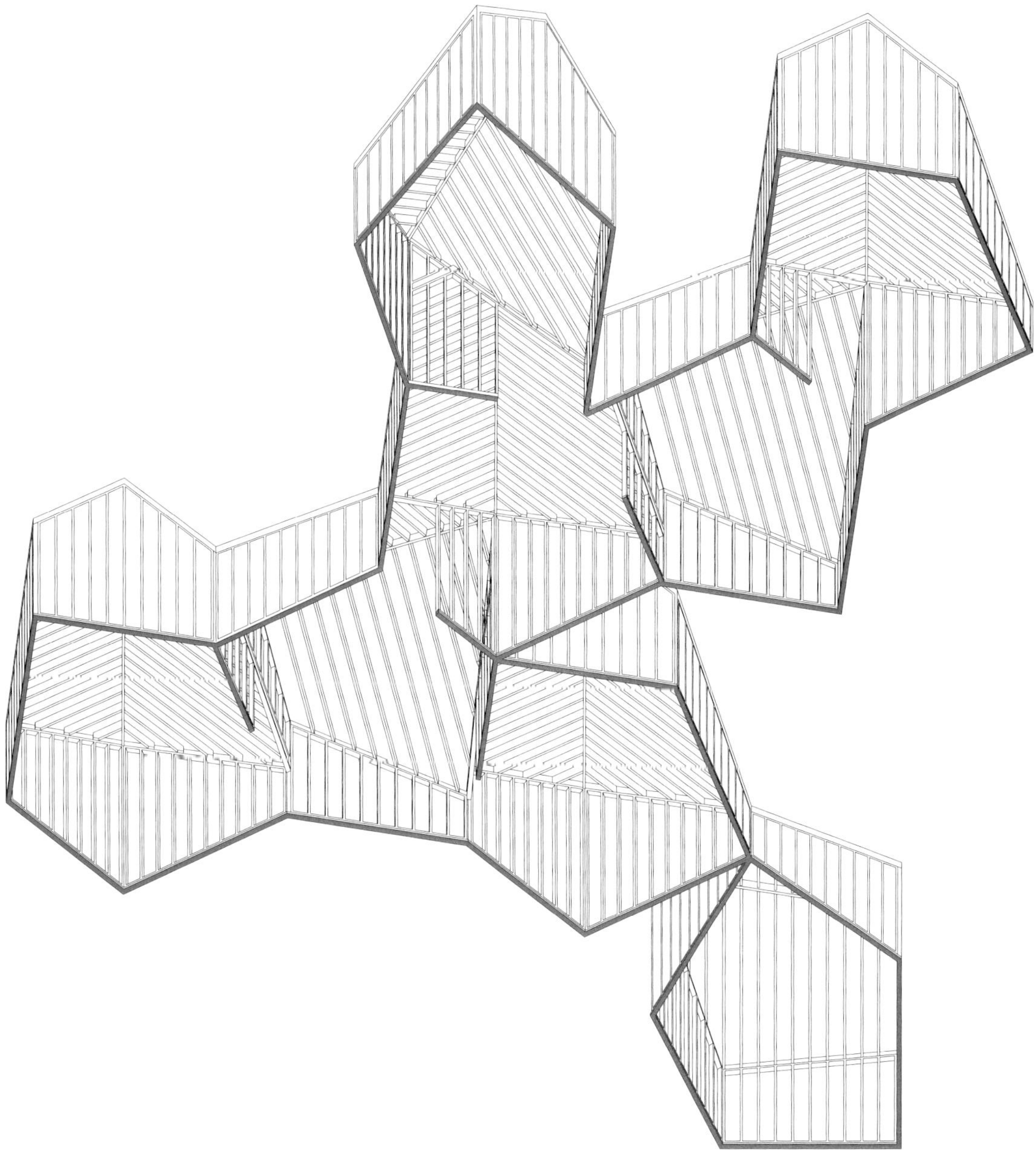

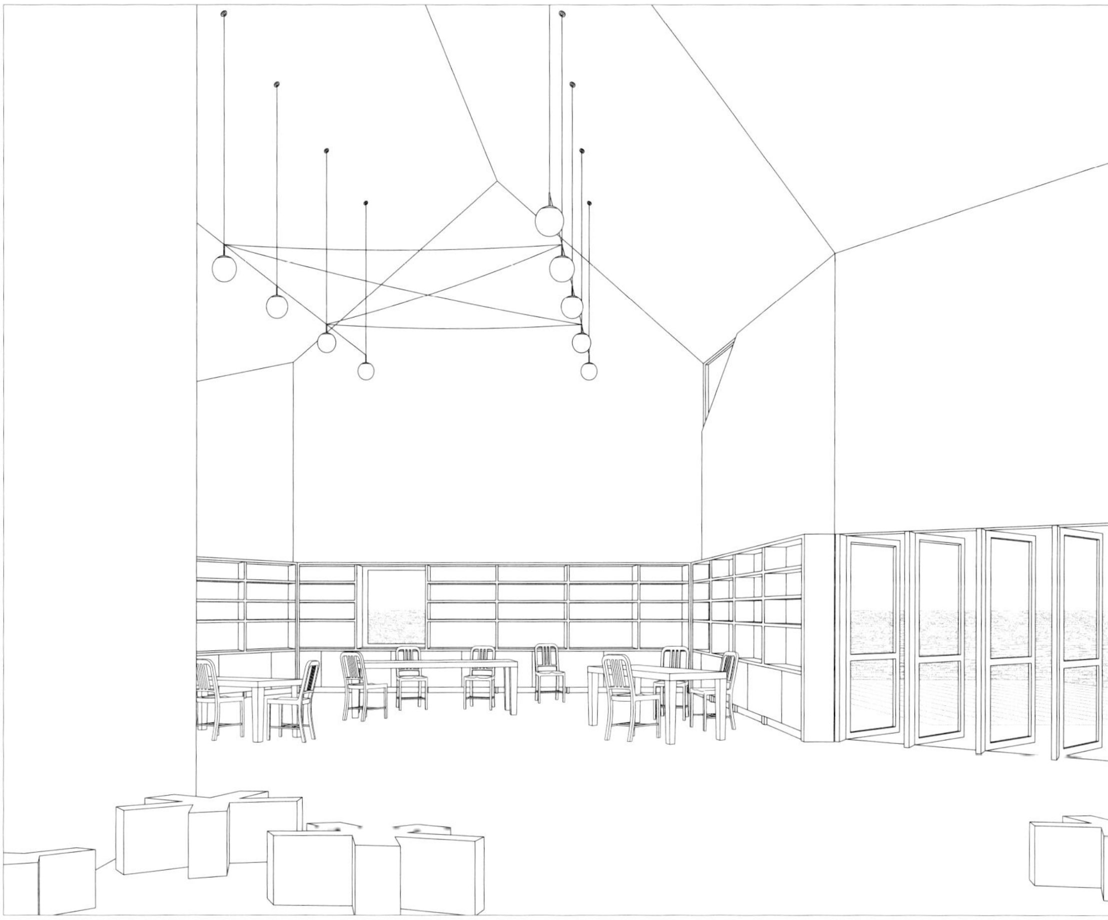

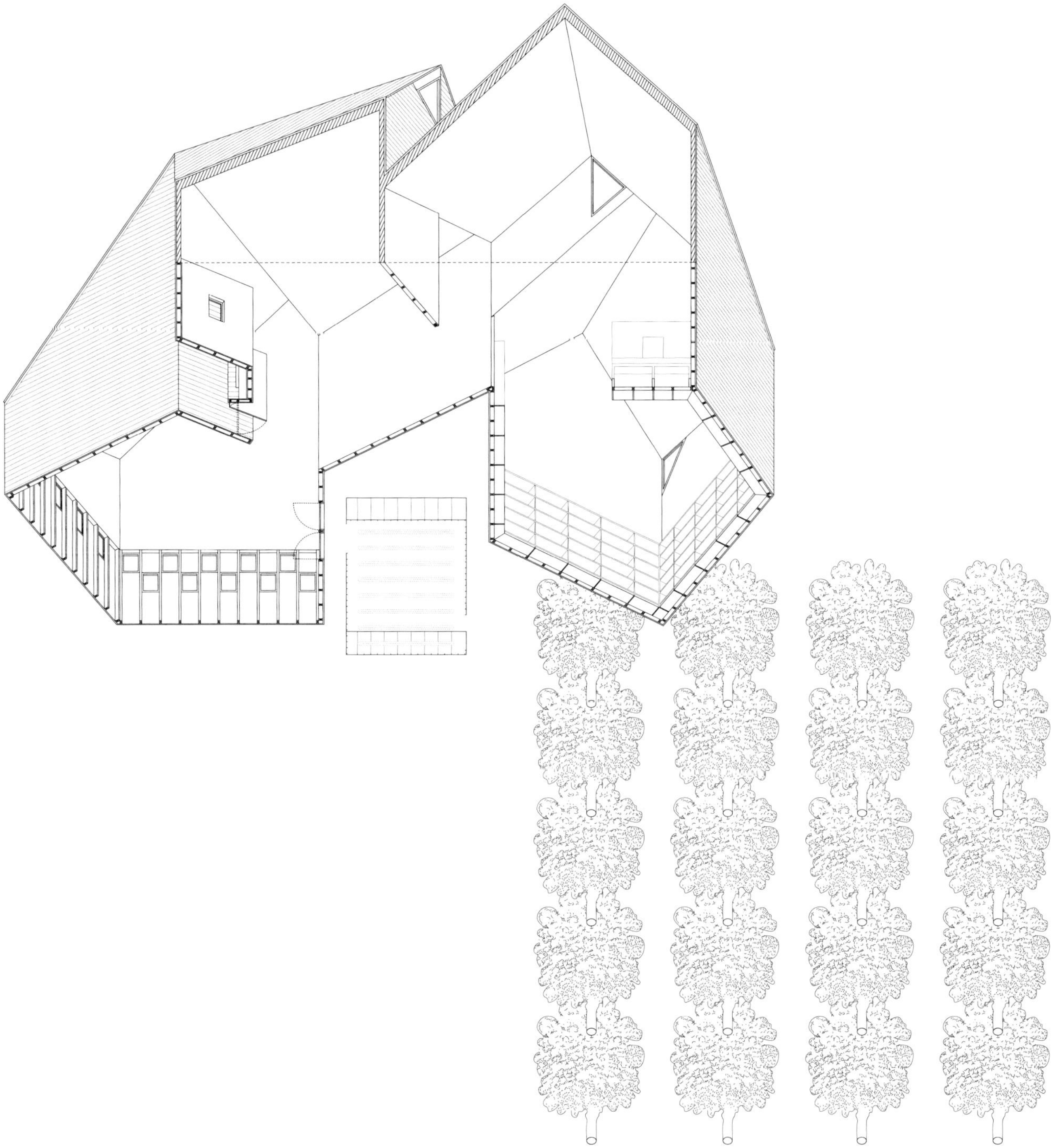

One Step Removed: Reflections on Some Drawings by Stan Allen

Helen Thomas

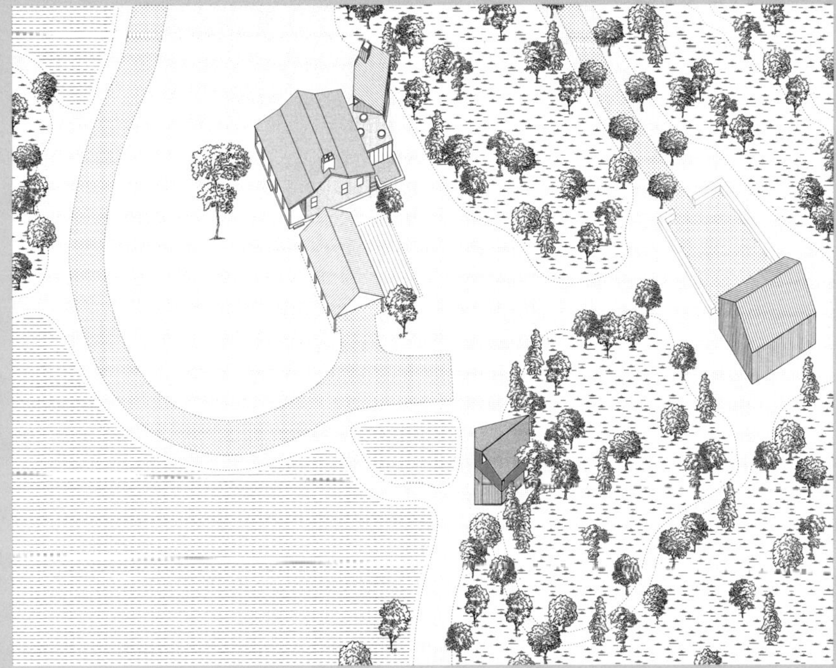

E/V House & Studio, site axonometric

The forest floods the page from the east, lapping around the simplest form; dark lines define a plain rectangular block with a pitched roof, paler parallel lines the texture of its cladding, their spacing suggesting shadow or a change in aspect rather than perspective. The frills of tree branches touch the other two members of a loose ensemble sited on the forest's boundary with a grassy meadow. Although their presence in the reality of the project is intense and atmospheric, imprinting itself in shadows and reflections on the pale surfaces of the buildings, changing through the seasons, the trees are depicted as individual figures, like old-fashioned Letraset transfers that have been carefully rubbed onto the surface of the paper. These suggest the different species that make up the forest, mostly of the deciduous category, and are irregularly dispersed over a uniform field of symbols depicting undergrowth. The strangeness of these repetitive tufts of grass is nothing compared with the open pasture that meets the woodland's margins, which is shown as a field of parallel lines alternating with rows of even dashes. If this is a site plan, what it reveals about the site it reveals about the architecture, an architecture that is American in all its fundamental characteristics.

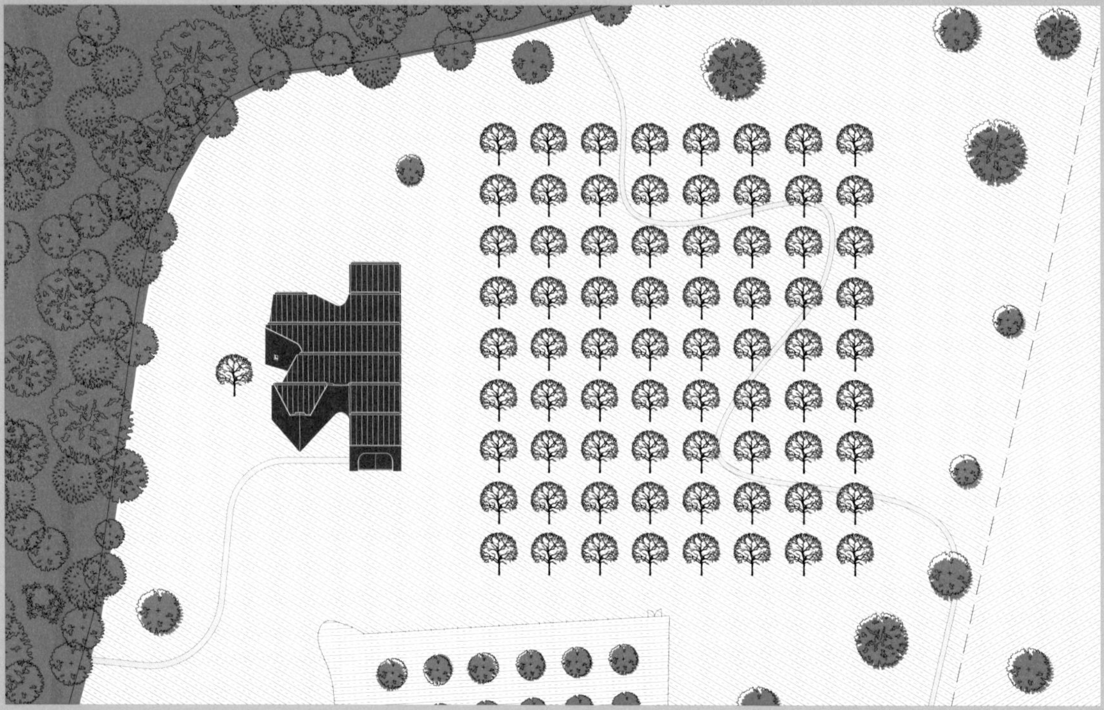

Olana Orchard Studio, site axonometric (homage to Stanley Tigerman's Hot Dog House)

The site plan as an axonometric replete with coded patterns, such as that for the Hudson River Studio described above, recurs in the drawings of Stan Allen. Another example is that for the Olana Orchard Studio, this time named as such; although again, the label for the drawing cannot capture the ambiguity of the collaged techniques. Here the trees at the forest edge are drawn in plan, their natural dishevelment expressed in neat overlapping circumferences. The building, the only element drawn in axonometric but with a mysterious dark surface,[1] fronts a grid of leafless trees that are shown in elevation; this constitutes the orchard. Whether it is a sign of an orchard—"a screen of signs and formulas"[2]—or a true measurement of the size and extent of an actual place is difficult to discern. This equivocal technique of representation is symptomatic of the relationship between the empirical and the conceptual qualities of the buildings on their sites. In this current iteration of Allen's practice in the Hudson River Valley, a refocusing on the smaller scale that began during the period of his field theory work, he identifies generating principles that emerge from what he calls a rule-based process.[3] Even though Allen has been closely engaged in the construction processes of these projects,[4] his deliberate and self-consciously intellectual approach separates the products of design from their place in a way that is essentially American, even when reflected in Europe.[5]

An architectural drawing is already one step away from the reality of a building, an intellectual pursuit carried out remotely from the site of its construction. The bodily labor of craft and construction is separated from the conceptual work of art, and drawing is a means through which intentions are imagined, resolved, and communicated. Historically, the second step away from the visceral was taken almost simultaneously with the first,[6] and is embodied in the beginning of America, as argued by Mexican philosopher Edmundo O'Gorman in his book *The Invention of America*. Because it exists in a colonized land, there is no possibility of the autochthonous in American culture: "it will be necessary to reconstruct history," O'Gorman wrote, "not of the discovery of America, *but rather the idea that America was discovered*, which is not the same."[7]

Conventionally, America and Europe share a continuous history and geography. For example, in his discussion of the forest edge, symbolic of the frontier since the time of the pilgrims,[8] Robert Geddes, who like Allen is a former dean of Princeton University School of Architecture, looked, without question, to the European classical as a starting point in architectural terms. n his reflections upon Marc-Antoine Laugier's engraving of the primitive hut (1755), Geddes proposed that the meeting of grassland and woodland provided the ideal location for architecture's invention and production out of a natural world.[9]

O'Gorman's statement challenges the concept of the frontier that presupposes a primeval and sublime American wilderness, equivalent to classical nature in its original state (although it could be argued that that, too, had been colonized); it was already an invented landscape within which a European architecture had to be transformed in response. O'Gorman proposed that "what one should ask of America is an *authentic* life even if it is not autochthonous."[10] An American architecture that denies the colonizing move and claims an autochthonous vernacular cannot be authentic, as Edith Wharton's *Hudson River Bracketed* character Halo Spear points out: "Hudson River Bracketed" is the "indigenous style of architecture in this part of the world"—the Hudson River Valley where Allen's projects are mostly located—and it consists of "[. . .] architectural elements ingeniously combined from the Chinese and the Tuscan."[11]

This tension between the myth of an empty land from which an American vernacular could grow and the fact of its invention imbues Allen's thesis of the "situated objects," in which the issue of authenticity lies at the core. As a starting point, he quotes Donald Judd: "Things that exist exist, and everything is on their side."[12] In effect, Allen invents his own twenty-first century vernacular, and he too cites the Doric.

W/H House, montage

The backdrop is a curtain of trees. Deep shadows are flattened into unevenly shaped but monotone patches of dense ink, given presence in contrast to the pixelated absence of color, depicting light pouring into the forest and dripping down the branches and trunks to splash on the ground where it turns to grass. In front, a smooth, featureless plane overlaps this image, its crudely cut edges modified only in front of the "render,"[13] where the ink seems to have been brushed up by fine bristles to mask the hole it is dug into. The luminous house is an alien object, but it seems to conjure a vernacular familiar in rural hamlets and villages. The roof is pitched, after all, with a shadow suggesting a shallow overhanging eve. The woodiness of the surroundings is embodied in it—a little stove chimney pokes up at the back, for example, and the horizontal lines on the facades suggest a timber cladding over a simple frame. It is of its place, but an uncanny inhabitant.

"There's something else informing this work," explained Allen in a 2017 Princeton lecture, "a concept originally articulated by Demetri Porphyrios, which has been expanded on by Kenneth Frampton: the notion of Doricism. It was originally used by Porphyrios to talk about Scandinavian Classicism—it's a moment in which the classical and the vernacular coincide." He continued with some examples: "I see the same austere sensibility in this Shaker interior, and of course the extraordinary Resurrection Chapel by Lewerentz at the Woodland Cemetery. There's a weird tension in these blank facades, all of the proportions are slightly off, and of course if you know the project, the portico is in the wrong place." The Doric is not an element in a well-known language of architecture, but an oscillating state made static. In this definition, its essential qualities come from the relationship between its inert and seemingly immutable presence and the interesting unlikeliness of its existence.

K/S Library, montage

This time there is an existing building, and it is not just equal to the natural components of the landscape, it is the same thing. It seems to enact Judd's text, which Allen quotes, as it continues, "Everything is equal, just existing, and the values and interests they have are only adventitious."[14] The old house is trapped in a web of shadows that belong to the trees, repeated on the ground, and defining the mysterious realm behind the thresholds of door and windows that prowls in the depths of the undergrowth. The skin of the building belongs to the sky and the sunshine on the sloping lawn. Again, the image is constructed purely of darkness and light, except for the "render," which is pinned down by the trunk of a tree, unable to escape. It twists and writhes, though, its faceted planes depicted through darker tones generated by the same light source as the background, which make it look more like a model shot pasted in. This hand-made character is deceiving, in an image built on the computer but simulating a different era when hand and mind were more closely connected.

M/M House & Studio, site axonometric

"It smells so inviting, a gem set in the wood.
Just fancy a night in a house made of food,
With walls to be biting and roofs to be chewed,
All over the icing Mama used to make,
Beneath that marzipan cottage a cake,
And then in a pen there are gingerbread men."[15]

A display of textures fires the imagination: irregularly speckled sheets jostling on the page; frilly, tangled mounds; slices neatly stacked in zigzag rows; little chunks of stripiness. It is a mirage evocative of the object of Hansel and Gretel's desire, a house made of sweets in the middle of the forest at the crossroad of paths on a difficult journey. Even the ground around the building has been corralled into a pen that hugs and separates its world from the outside void. In this drawing the conventional codes of material representation are subtly transformed, enough to dissolve the certainty of what they signify and to transfer the authority of interpretation from the author to the viewer. "Colonization was [. . .] a world-scale *coup de théâtre* which leaves deep, nostalgic traces everywhere [. . .]. For the Old World, it represents the unique experience of an idealized substitution of values, almost as you find in science-fiction novels,"[16] wrote Baudrillard.

So many parts tumble together: recognizably architectural forms, some from the typology of collective memory, all from different times, in a dense ensemble, and a floor like cracked nougat already tapped with a little hammer. Separated from the forest crowd two trees stand, like the two children looking in, trapped in a science-fictional account of past times. Fairy tales come from authorless oral traditions, and when written down there is usually an agenda and always a naming, capturing, and claiming of something previously fugitive and unowned. In the case of the tale of Hansel and Gretel it was that of the Brothers Grimm, "in pursuit of the authentic German *Geist*." In search of a means towards cultural unity, gathering folk stories from across Germany's principalities, they fastened the mutability of an oral tradition into written language, mimicking the Doric. In the fictional world of Allen's drawings, there is room for the potential reality, for the invention of its authenticity, to be made by the viewer—depending on how the signs are read and the perspective wrested from the author's vision.

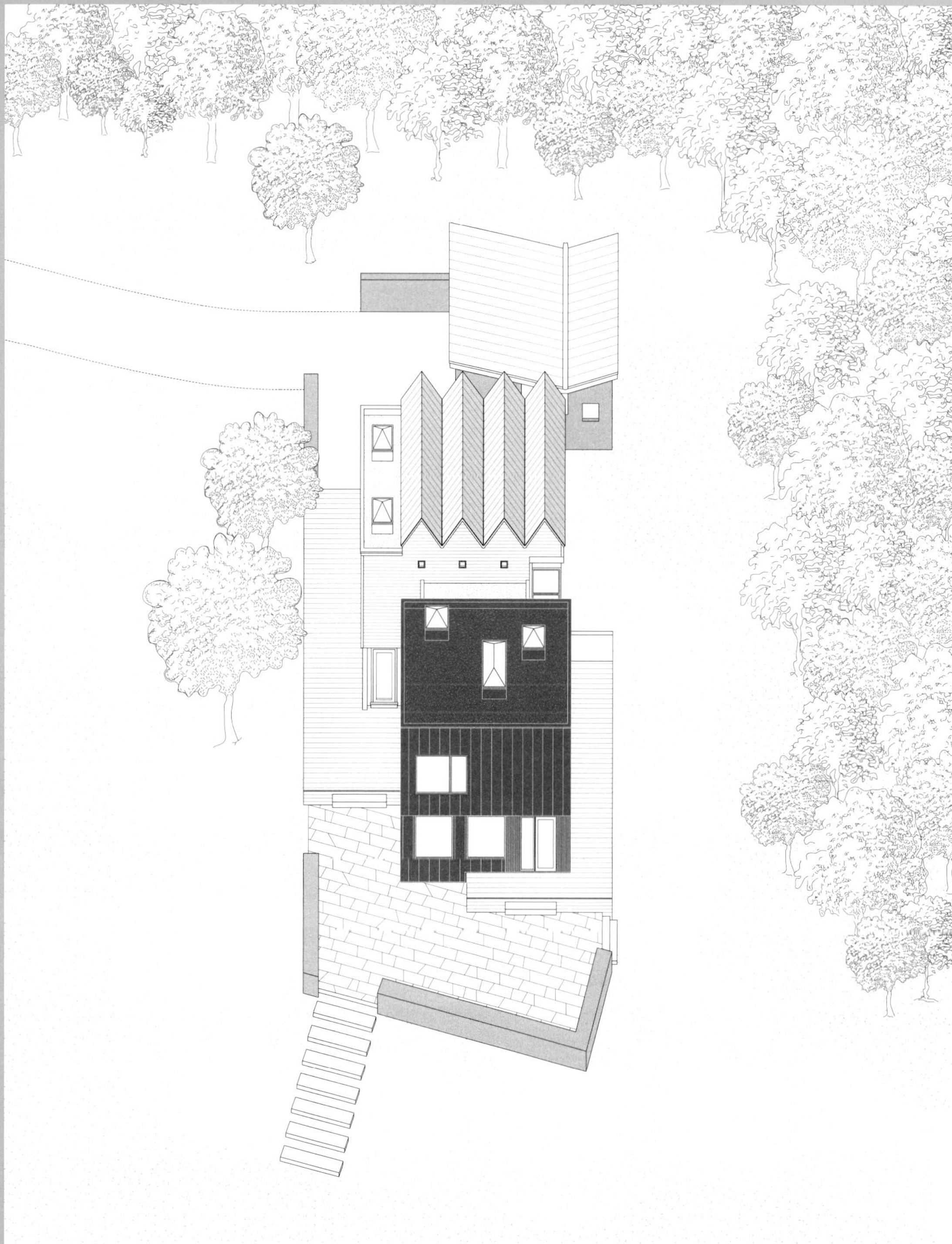

J/S House, site axonometric

1. See in this volume, Stan Allen, "Explaining by Drawing: In Axonometric", pp. 236–244, for insight into Allen's long engagement with and development of this projection and its expressive qualities. The version featured in the drawing "Olana Orchard Studio, site axonometric" can be seen as a quote of the axonometric drawings invented, themselves as quotes of John Hejduk and O. M Ungers, or *San Rocco* magazine, which adds a layer of complexity to its potential meaning.
2. Jean Baudrillard, *America* (London, New York: Verso, 1988, first published 1986), 56.
3. Stan Allen, "Situated Objects," lecture at Princeton School of Architecture, November 5, 2017, https://soa.princeton.edu/content/lecture-series%3A-stan-allen (last accessed July 20, 2020).
4. As Stan Allen describes in the introduction to this volume, pp. 8–15.
5. As Baudrillard observed in his mid-1980s travelogue across the United States: "The confrontation between America and Europe reveals not so much a *rapprochement* as a distortion, an unbridgeable rift. There isn't just a gap between us, but a whole chasm of modernity. You are born modern, you do not become so. And we have never become so." Baudrillard, op. cit., 73.
6. If the workshops of St. Peter's Basilica in Rome are taken as the site of transfer of the process of architectural design from the direction of the master craftsman to the architect's invention and its communication through drawing, then the dates are almost simultaneous: the construction of St. Peter's began in 1506, and America was first named on the 1507 maps of Martin Waldseemüller.
7. "[. . .] será necesario reconstruir la historia, no del descubrimiento de América, *sino de la idea de que América fue descubierta*, que no es lo mismo." Edmundo O'Gorman, *La Invención de América. Investigación acerca de la estructura histórica del Nuevo mundo y del sentido de su devenir* (Mexico City: Fondo de Cultura Económica, 1995, first published 1958), 17.
8. As Nathaniel Hawthorne in *The Scarlet Letter* (first published in 1850) makes clear, this frontier is intellectual and moral more than it is physical; a symbol far more potent than its tangible qualities.
9. Robert Geddes, "AD Profile 44 The Forest Edge," *Architectural Design* 52 (11–12), 1982, 2–23, here 3.
10. Edmundo O'Gorman, "Do the Americas Have a Common History?," *Points of View* 3, December 1941, 9.
11. Edith Wharton, *Hudson River Bracketed* (London: Virago, 2006, first published 1929), 66–67. Halo Spear is reading an extract from "A. J. Downing Esq. on Landscape Gardening in America," a reference by Wharton to the pattern books of the mid-nineteenth century by Downing himself, specifically *A Treatise on the Theory and Practice of Landscape Gardening, Adapted to North America*, 1841 and *Cottage Residences*, 1842, but also, for example, Calvert Vaux's architectural style book for the Hudson River School: *Villas and Cottages: A Series of Designs Prepared for Execution in the United States*, first published in 1852, two years after his arrival in the United States from Britain.
12. Donald Judd, "Black, White, and Gray," *Arts*, March 1964; he continues: "[. . .] Everything is equal, just existing, and the values and interests they have are only adventitious." See this volume, p. 8, for Allen's reference.
13. The architect refers to these drawings as "montages": the building elements are rendered in Rhino, and the image is composed in Photoshop.
14. Judd, op. cit.
15. Adelheid Wette, libretto for Engelbert Humperdinck's opera *Hansel and Gretel*; see the accompanying booklet in the 2007 Chandos Records Ltd recording of the Philharmonia Orchestra conducted by Charles Mackerras, 91.
16. Baudrillard, op. cit., 78.

NEW

TU

NA

RES

*"After seeing electricity, I lost interest in Nature.
Not up-to-date enough."*

Vladimir Mayakovsky

Interior Landscapes

Mies van der Rohe, Resor House, Jackson Hole, Wyoming, 1937, photomontage

Where do we look for nature today? The imperatives of climate change and global urbanization remind us that nature is everywhere and nowhere: a vast planetary system now in crisis. The archetypal idea of architecture as shelter has always implied separation and protection from nature. A building is a delimited precinct of artificial climate, by definition set apart from the hazards of climate and weather. Over time, developments in construction technology have enabled greater degrees of transparency in the building envelope, opening up visual access to the landscape while maintaining climactic separation.

Jennifer Steinkamp, *Blind Eye*, installation at the Clark Institute, Williamstown, MA, 2018

In the twentieth century, new techniques of steel construction and large-scale plate-glass manufacture allowed unprecedented visual transparency. The interior space of the house was opened up to light and view, transforming domestic space. What had been a space of retreat from nature became a framing device directed outwards at the landscape beyond. In an iconic photomontage of the Resor House (1937), Mies van der Rohe juxtaposes delicate steel columns and window mullions with the massive peaks of the Grand Teton Mountains. An expansive architectural space frames the vast landscape beyond, minimizing the foreground presence of the architecture. But if nature is in this way brought into the house, it is brought only as far as the surface of the glass itself. The vast western landscape is converted into a framed image, like a CinemaScope screen. This is nature mediated by architecture and visual technologies: painting, photography, film, and, later, the digital screen.

The modern, glass-walled house effectively challenged the traditional idea of the house as refuge. The space of the house was opened up to the natural world, and by exposing the interior to the public eye, expectations of comfort and privacy were undermined. Yet for the modern movement, nature remains distinct from the architecture itself: a pastoral setting for an abstract formal statement, or an image to be looked at.

Today, urban and rural are inextricably mixed, and the presence of mankind everywhere marked on the landscape. Even the most remote site on the planet is subject to man-made atmospheric disturbances. Public space is no longer exclusively vested in the civic common; the ubiquity of digital media and devices have

Alvar Aalto, Paimio Sanatorium, Paimio, Finland, 1932

blurred the distinction between public and private life, and between the artificial and the man-made. Today, we understand landscape not as a framed object but as an immersive field. An emerging sensibility in recent art and architecture has begun to blur the boundary between inside and outside, working with ambiguous interior spaces that identify nature not with greenery or biomorphic form but with expansive interior spaces.

And so, if the grand narrative of the twentieth century was the progress of technology, architecture's challenge for this new century will surely be to come to terms with mankind's fraught relationship to nature, and to recognize the complete interpenetration of nature and culture in today's urbanized society. Nature is no longer something out there to be viewed, or a distant wilderness to be visited in passing. Instead it becomes part of our most intimate, everyday interior landscapes—one among many artificial natures.

"A cultivated man," Adolf Loos once said, "does not look out of the window." Confronting a century-long legacy of literal and phenomenal transparencies, these projects work with interiority not as a gesture of retreat but as a different form of engagement with nature. Rather than focus on a distant prospect of the natural world "out there," they reorient the gaze inwards, to partially closed worlds and expansive interior spaces. Rather than presenting nature as an object to be observed, at a distance, these spaces are permeated with indirect light and oblique views: skylights, pinholes, or cut-out windows. They mark a shift in understanding nature as pictured landscape to an understanding of nature as atmosphere, in its expansive, always changing, climatic context.

Richard L. McElhiney Architect, with Steven Vannort, J/S House,
Gallatin, NY, existing house, 1988

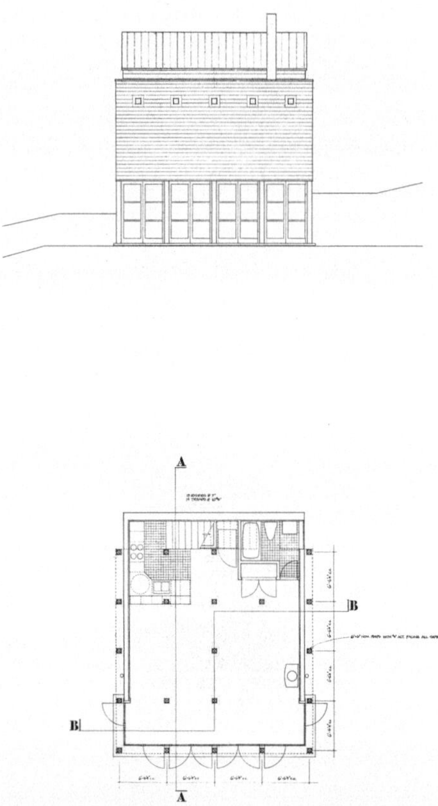

Plan and front elevation: existing house

Section and side elevation: existing house

Stan Allen Architect, J/S House

1. J/S HOUSE

The original structure on site, completed in 1989, was an artist live/work studio, designed by Richard L. McElhiney in collaboration with the artist client Steven Vannort. Sitting on a rounded hillock and wood plinth, the building had an unsettling aspect: a blank white box, punctuated by small square windows, floating on thin columns over an open-plan living area. It had a serrated roofline and a large bank of north-facing windows hidden from the road. Over time the studio, which had been modified for residential use, had fallen into disrepair.

The current owners are art collectors. Our brief was to double the size of the house, creating living space, a gallery for their collection, and a new second-floor bedroom overlooking the Roeliff Jansen Kill and the valley beyond. We studied many variations before deciding that the best way to complement the uncanny presence of the original, with its distinctive roofline, would be a simple box. Metal siding marks it out as something new. The figural energy comes from the existing building, and our task was to create a neutral counterpoint, in dialogue with the original, to form a new whole.

While the interior appears seamless, it required surgical precision to insert new steel supports to create the current, light-filled interior, free of columns. Detail and material difference are systematically suppressed in order to minimize the everyday clutter of domestic life. This is a space about living with art. The architectural presence lies in abstract space, light, and view, and the calibration of measure, rhythm, orientation, and movement.

Stan Allen Architect, J/S House; construction shoring

Frederic Church, *Clouds over Olana*, oil sketch

Frederic Church's: Olana, Hudson, NY.
Photo: Stan Allen

2. OLANA ORCHARD STUDIO

An invitation to exhibit at the Olana State Historic Site—the house and landscape constructed by painter Frederic Church overlooking the Hudson River—presented a unique opportunity to reflect on architecture's relationship to landscape and nature today. Working on site between 1860 and 1874, Church constructed an expansive and integrated complex of architecture and landscape that complemented his painterly vision of nature. The use of filtered light and carefully calibrated views turned the house into a device for viewing the landscape beyond: both the foreground that he designed and planted, and the larger ecological context of the Hudson River and Catskill mountains. One lesson Church learned from his close reading of the writings of Alexander von Humboldt was to see nature as a complex whole; the way in which the landscape views interpenetrate the space of the house is fully consistent with that idea.

Our proposal imagines that Olana will build a modest facility on the historic site for artists-in-residence: painters, sculptors, architects, or writers who could reflect on the legacy of the Hudson River School, local and regional ecologies, architecture, and landscape. Located below and out of sight of the main house, adjacent to the farmhouse and orchard, it has an indirect relationship to the historic site. It finds its place alongside the original working farm and restored orchards, at the edge of an open meadow. The building has an almost indifferent relationship to the site. It does not frame exterior space or interact with the landscape; neither does it command views from a high point, as the Church-designed house does. Instead, it forms a somewhat eccentric figure imposed on the working landscape.

Fully accepting the artificial nature of the architectural envelope, our proposal looks not outward but inward, as an alternative model both to the transparency of the glass curtain wall and the filtered transitional spaces of Church's architecture. The pavilion creates an immersive, light-filled interior that will serve as a living, working, and exhibition space. It is a shadowless space, with no right-angled corners, lit exclusively by north-light skylights, which concentrate the view on the sky and clouds, and the stars at night.

Stan Allen Architect, Olana Orchard Studio; model.
Photo: Stan Allen

J/S HOUSE

2018

Gallatin, NY

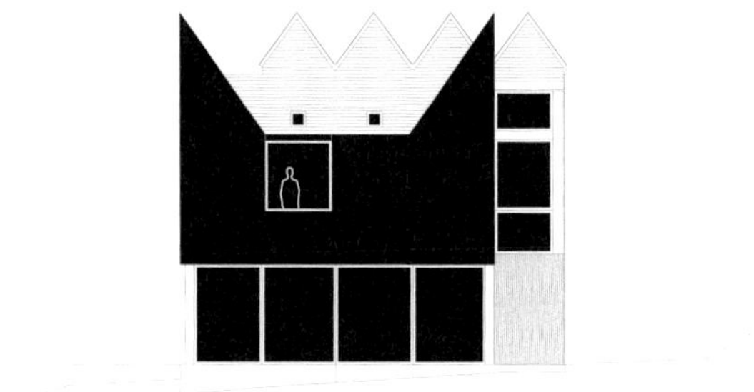

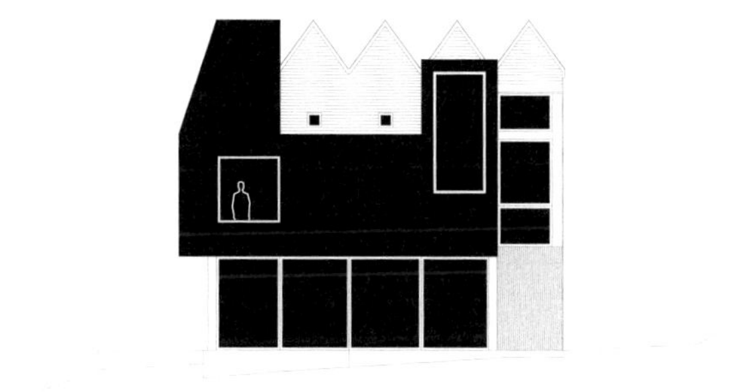

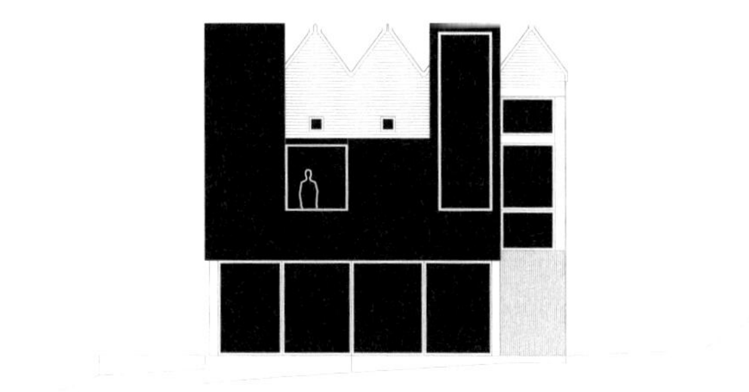

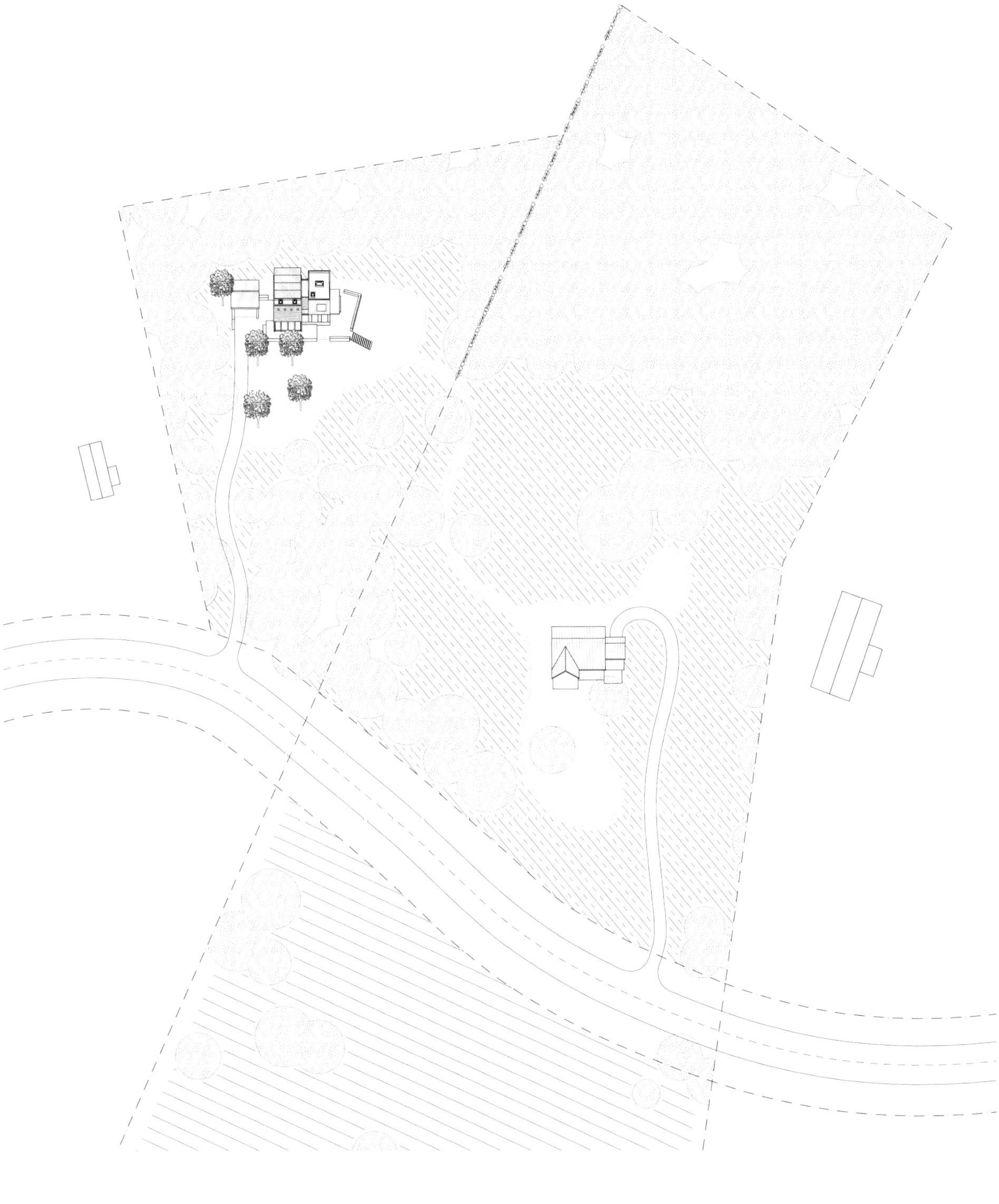

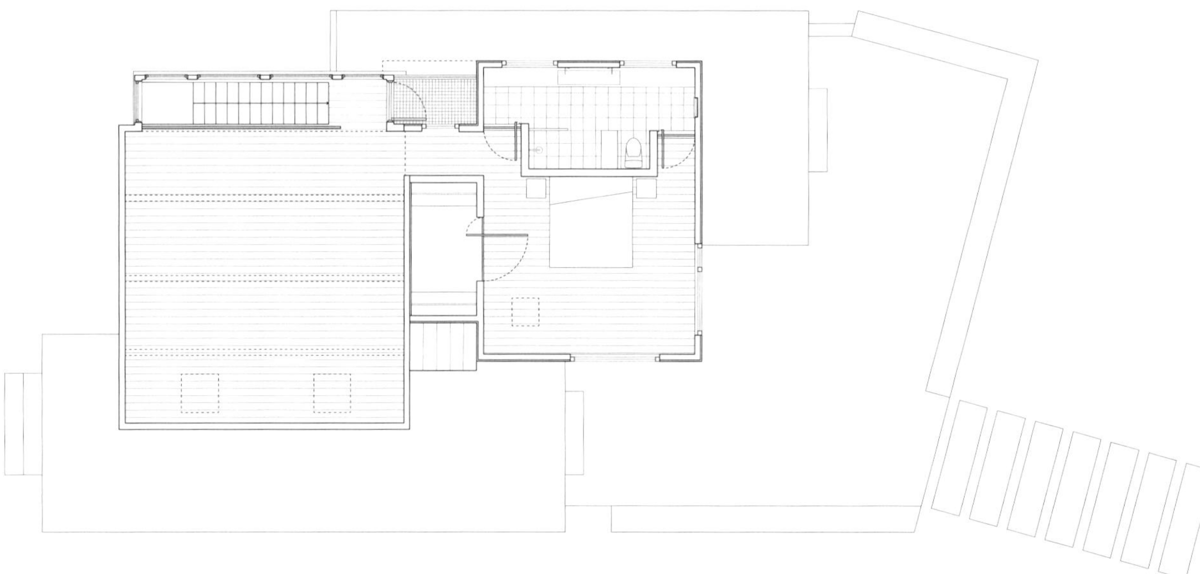

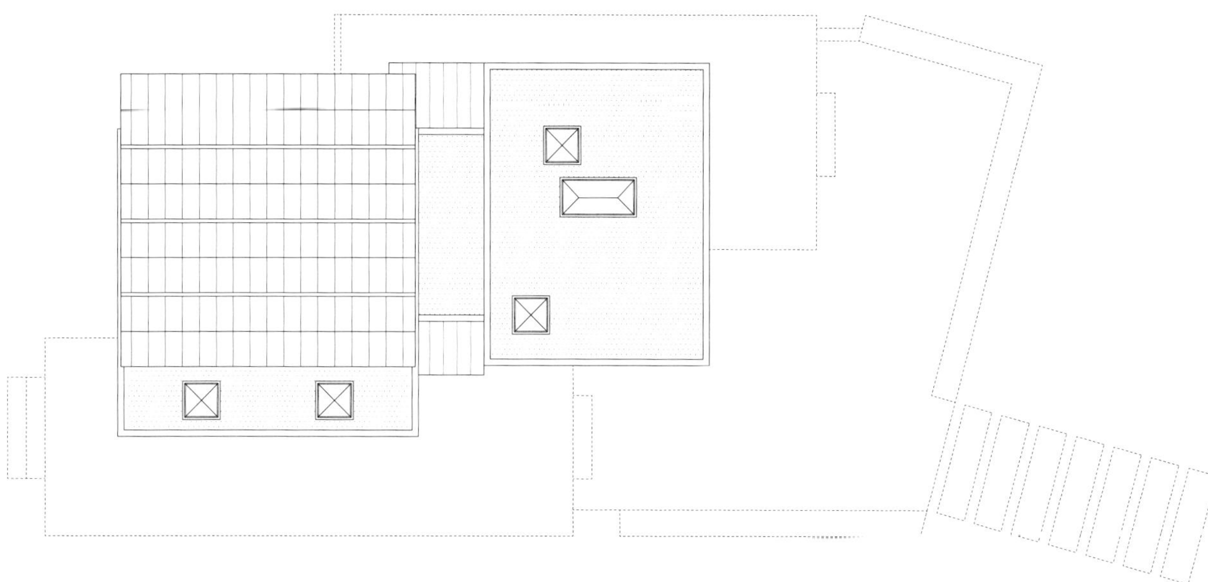

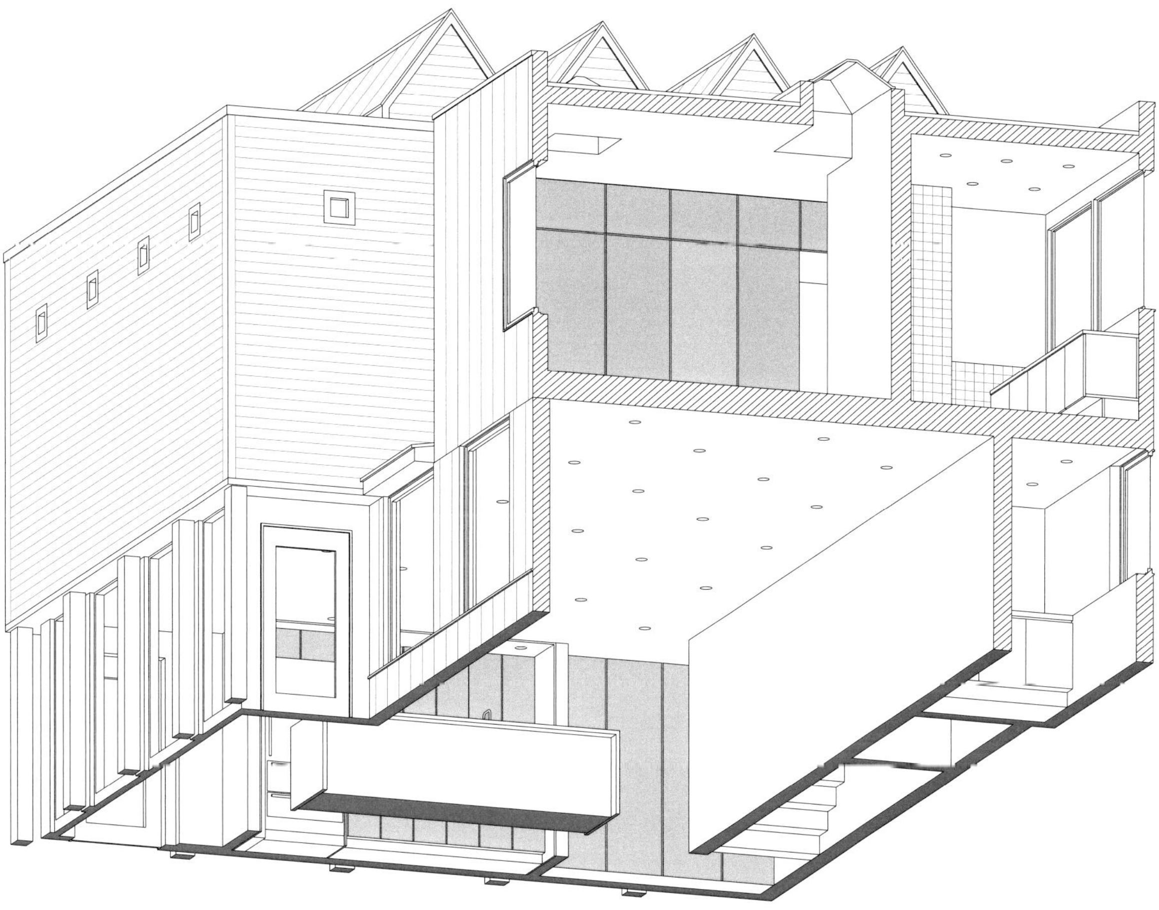

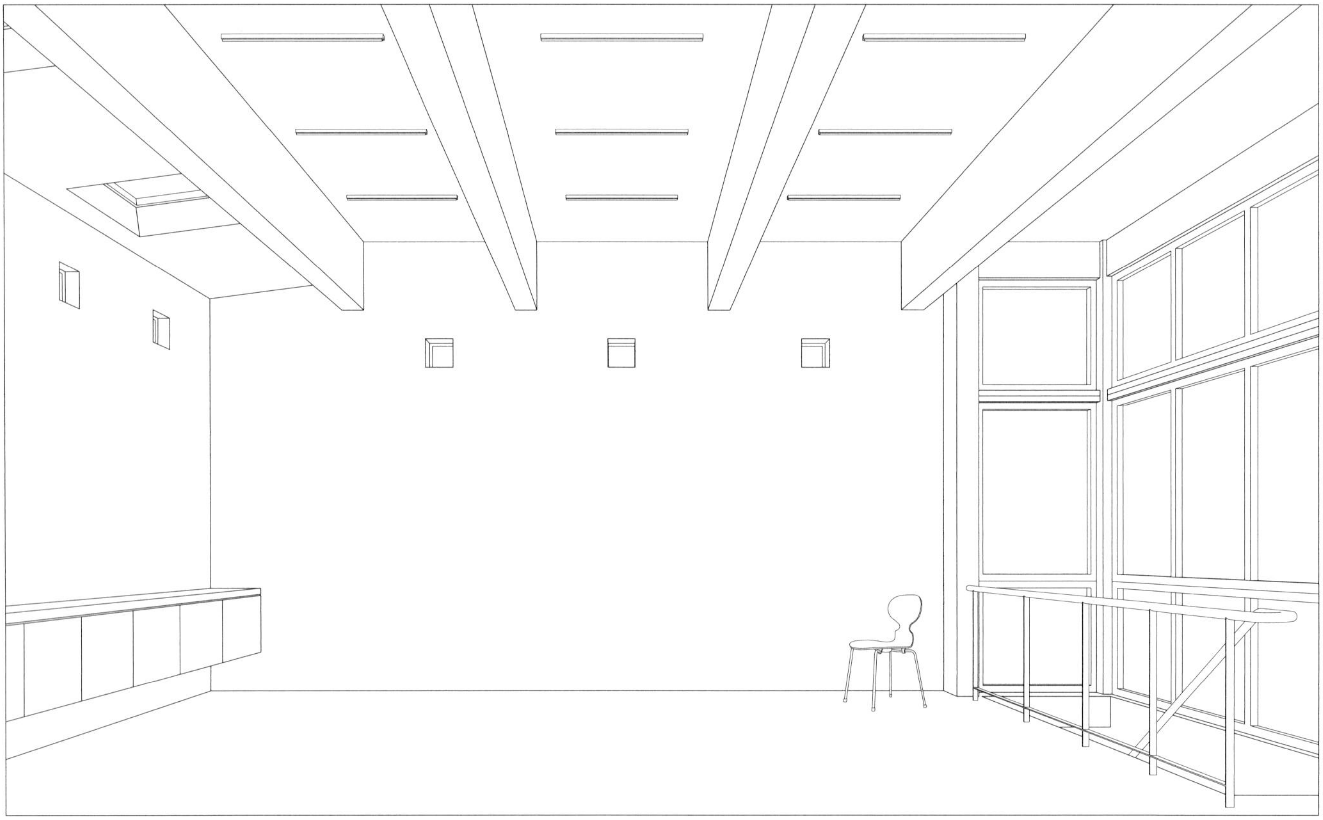

OLANA ORCHARD STUDIO

2019

Hudson, NY

Extruded plan form

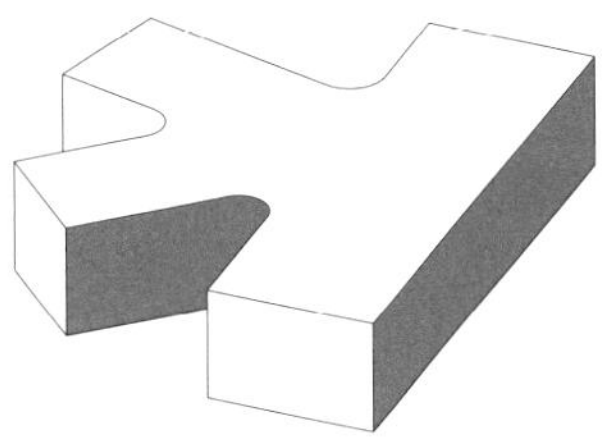

Cutting profile

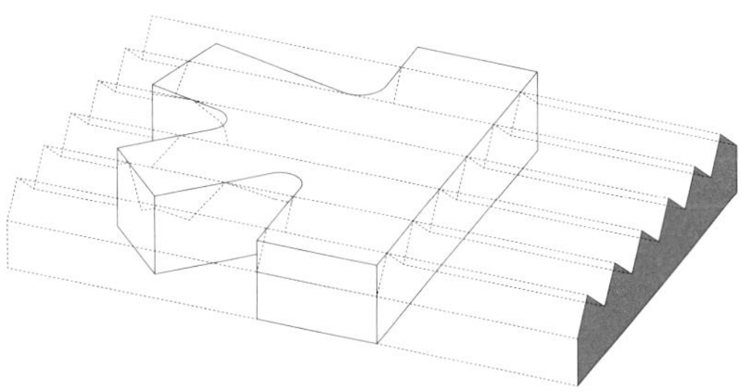

Composite object

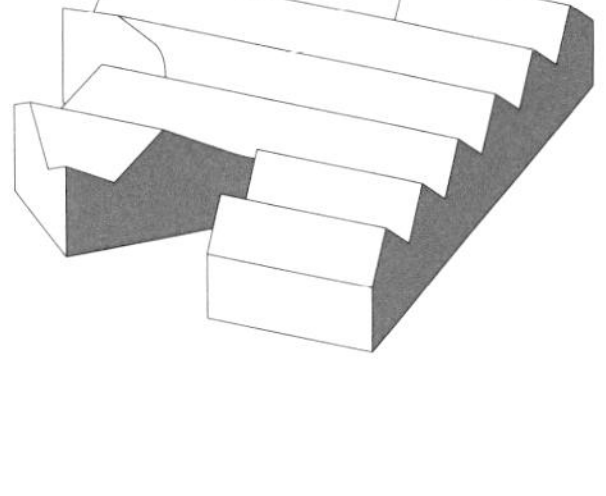

Quarry Hill
South Road
South Entrance
Kaaterskill Falls_Thomas Cole_1826
Red Hill
Lake
Farm Road
Cottage
Farm and C
Garden
Barnyard
Swamp
Swamp
O R
Crown Hill
Cultivated Ground

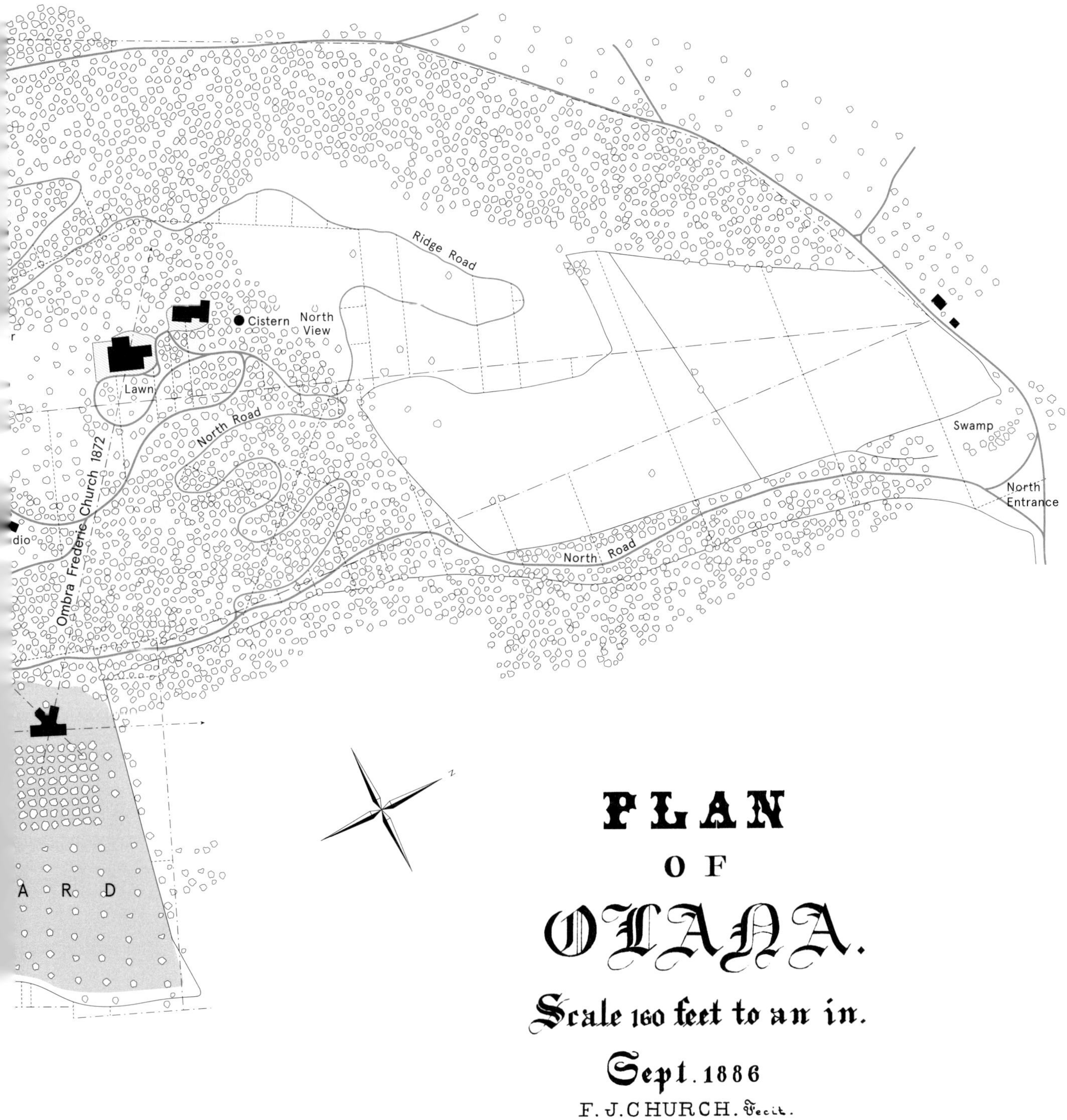

Ridge Road
Cistern
North View
Lawn
North Road
Ombra Frederic Church 1872
Swamp
North Entrance
North Road
PLAN
OF
OLANA.
Scale 160 feet to an in.
Sept. 1886
F. J. CHURCH. Fecit.

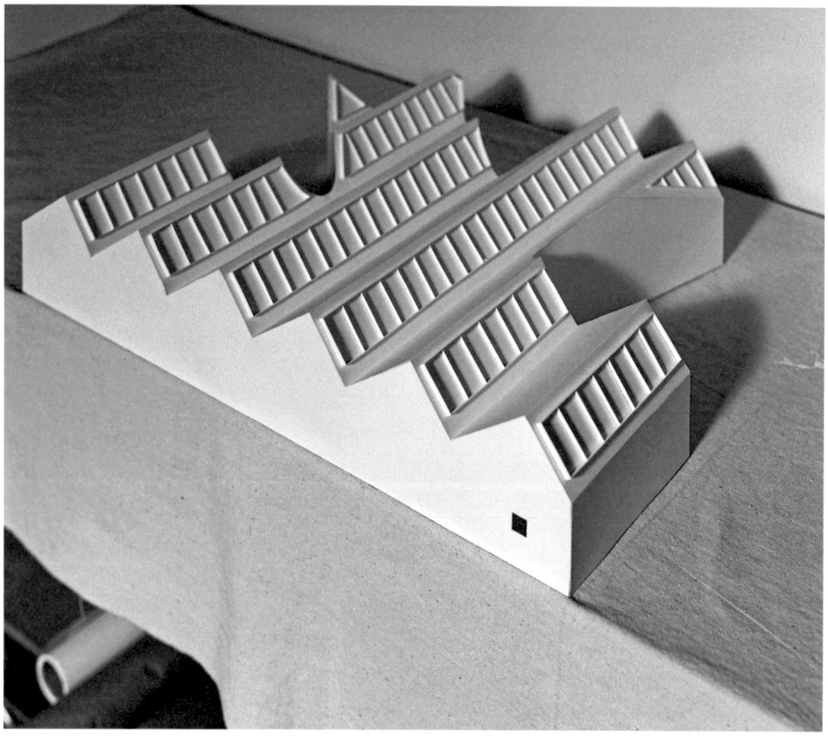

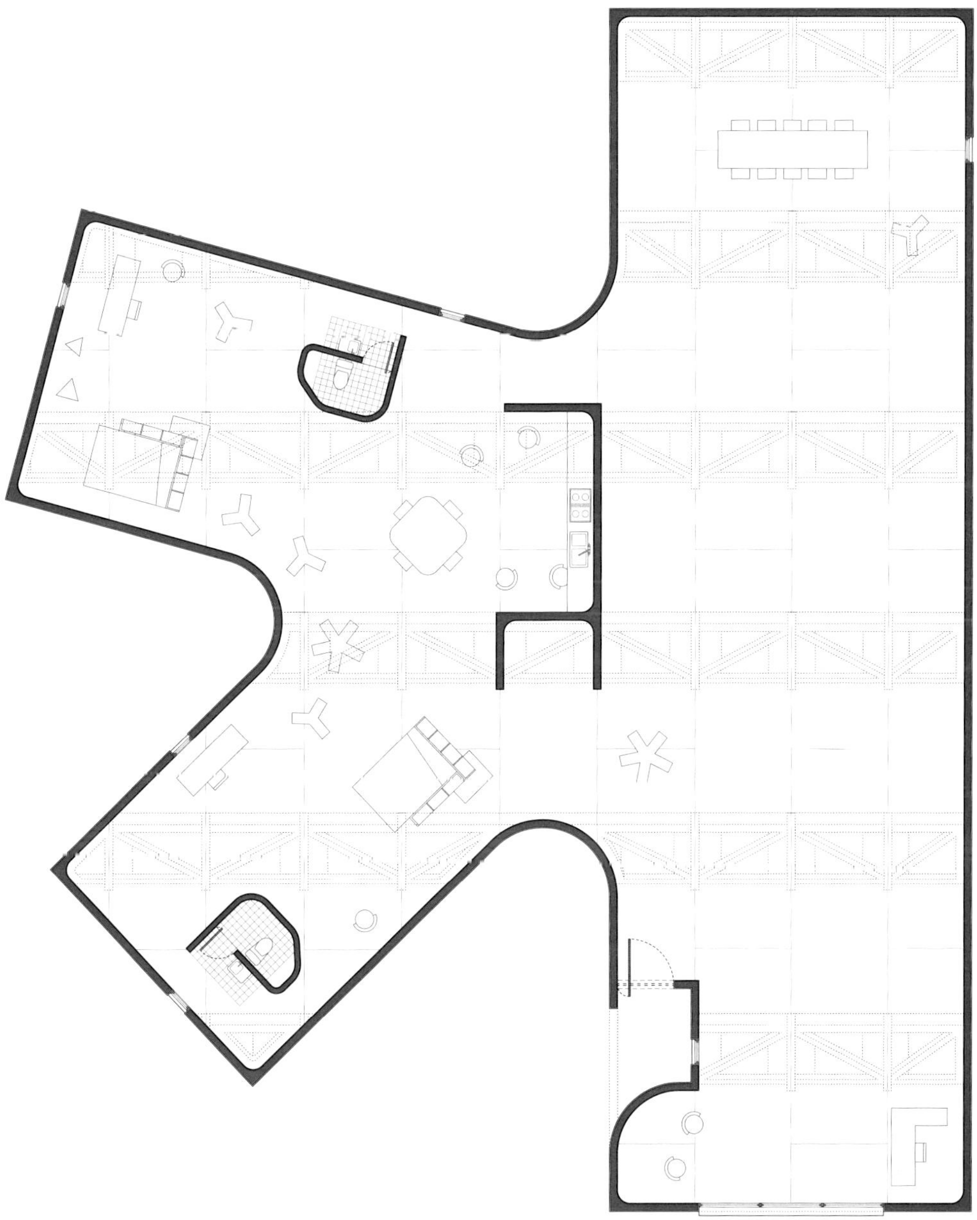

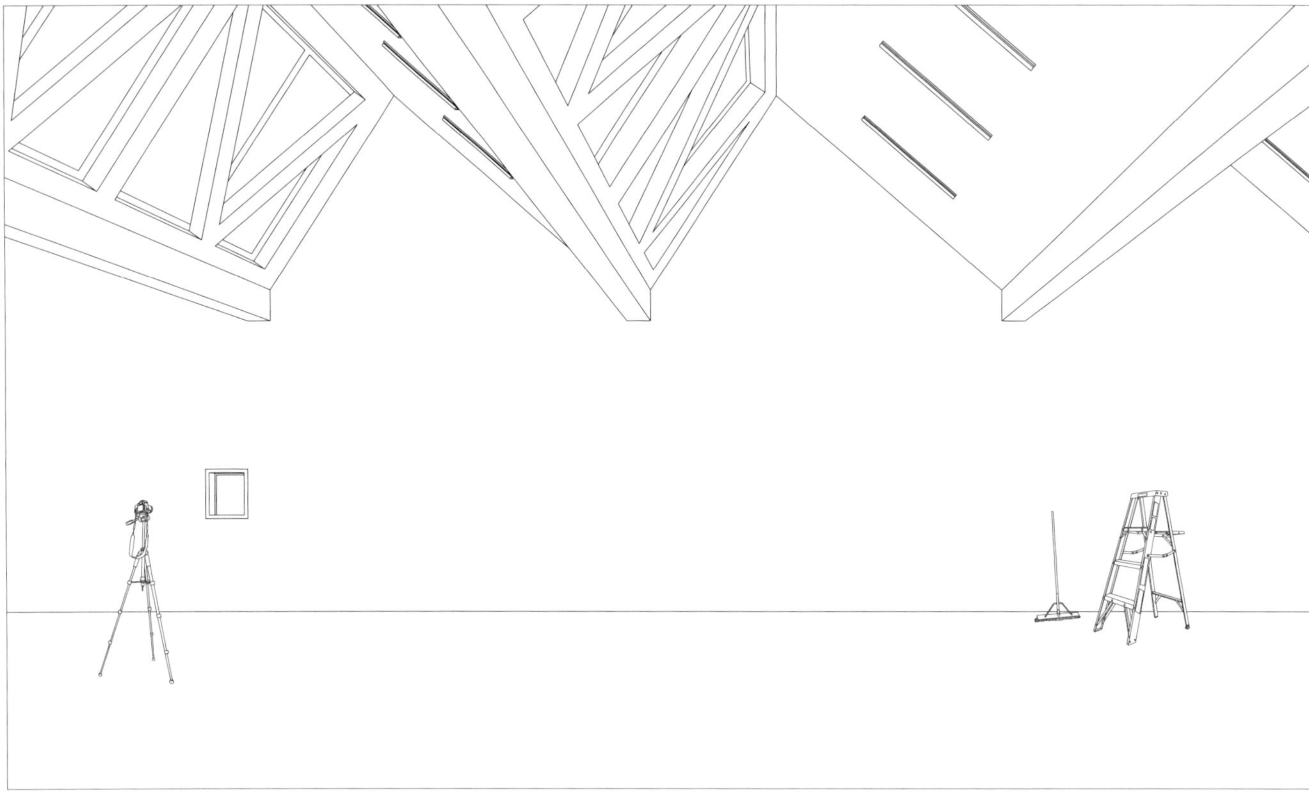

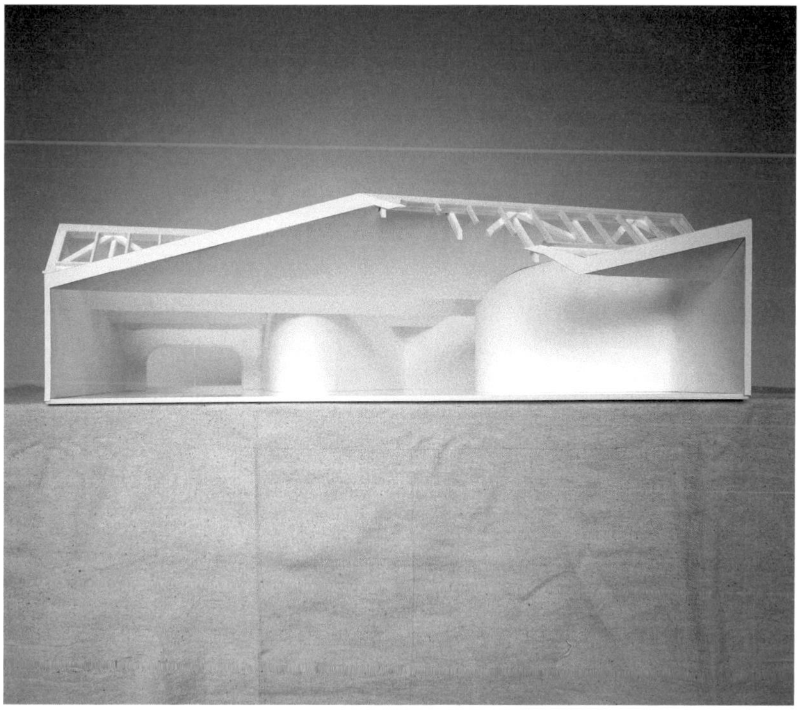

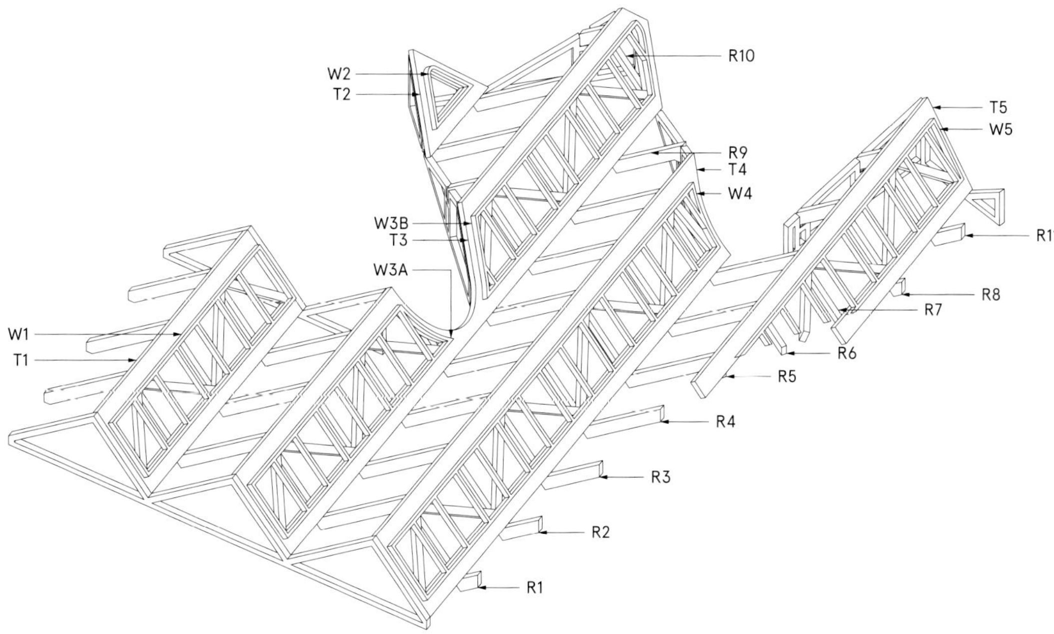
R10
W2
T2
T5
W5
R9
T4
W4
W3B
T3
R11
W3A
R8
R7
W1
T1
R6
R5
R4
R3
R2
R1

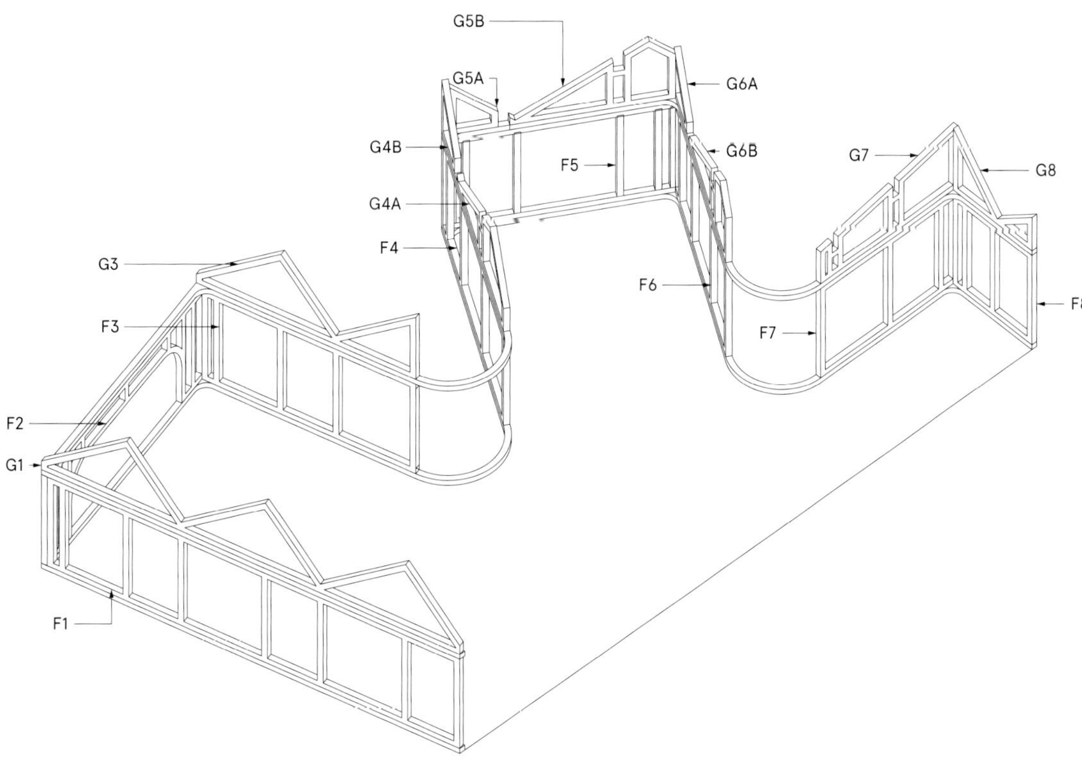
G5B
G5A
G6A
G4B
G6B
F5
G7
G8
G4A
F4
G3
F6
F8
F3
F7
F2
G1
F1

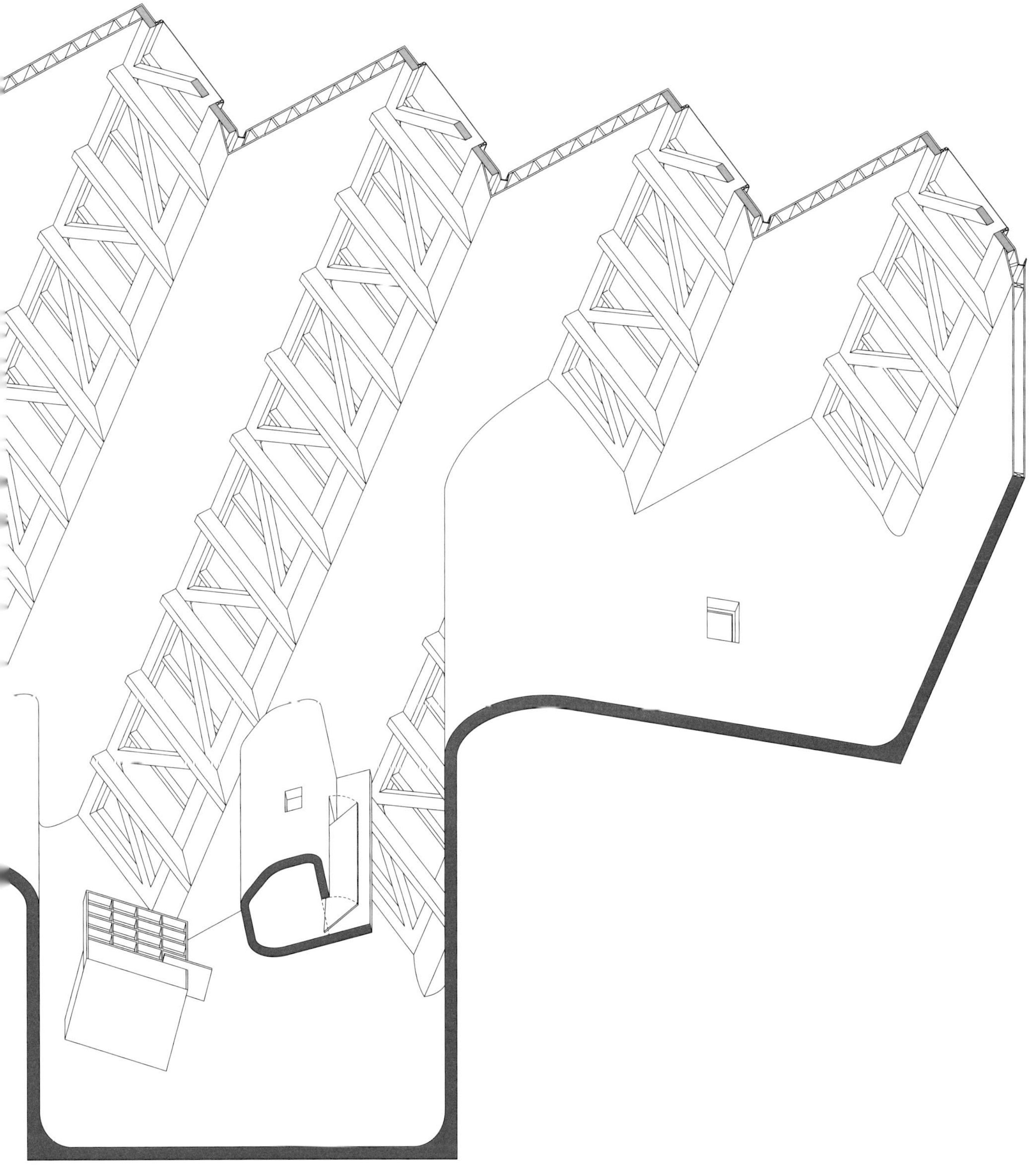

*"The plan determines everything;
it is the decisive moment."*

Le Corbusier

Explaining by Drawing: In Axonometric

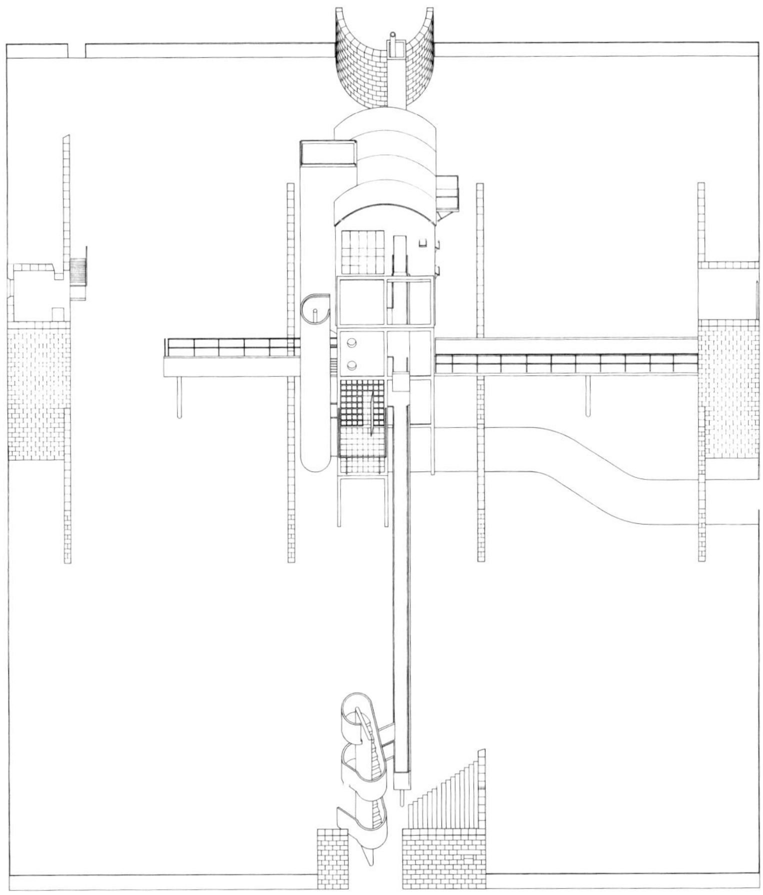

Stan Allen, Shinkenchiku Residential Design Competition, 1981; 90-degree projection, pencil on vellum

There are many forms of the axonometric, but the simplest to construct is a vertical projection from a rotated plan. This means that the plan geometries are preserved, while the elevations are skewed, maintaining dimensional consistency on an angled plane. The building is presented as an object, floating in abstract, measurable space. The viewer and vanishing point are both located at an infinite distance. But axonometrics have a pictorial quality,

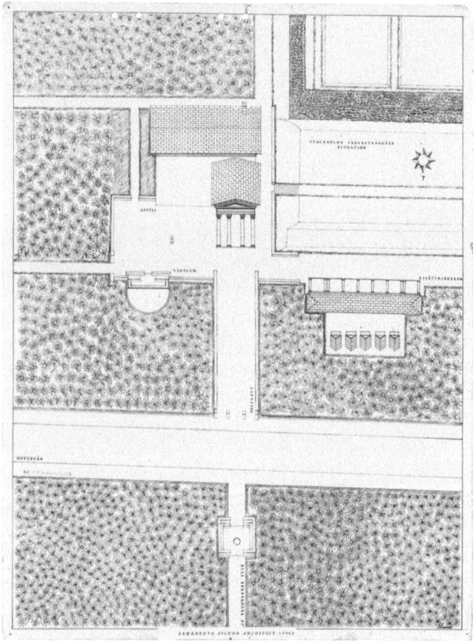

Sigurd Lewerentz, plan elevation of the Resurrection Chapel, Woodland Cemetery Stockholm, c. 1925

Stanley Tigerman, Hot Dog House, Harvard, IL, 1974; 90-degree projection,

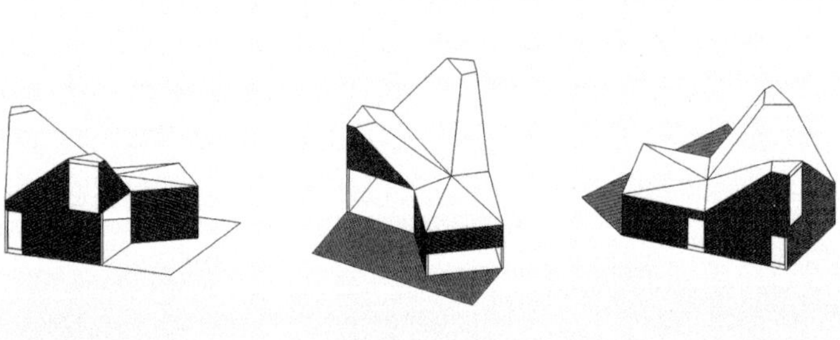

Stan Allen Architect, K/S Library; axonometric studies, 2016

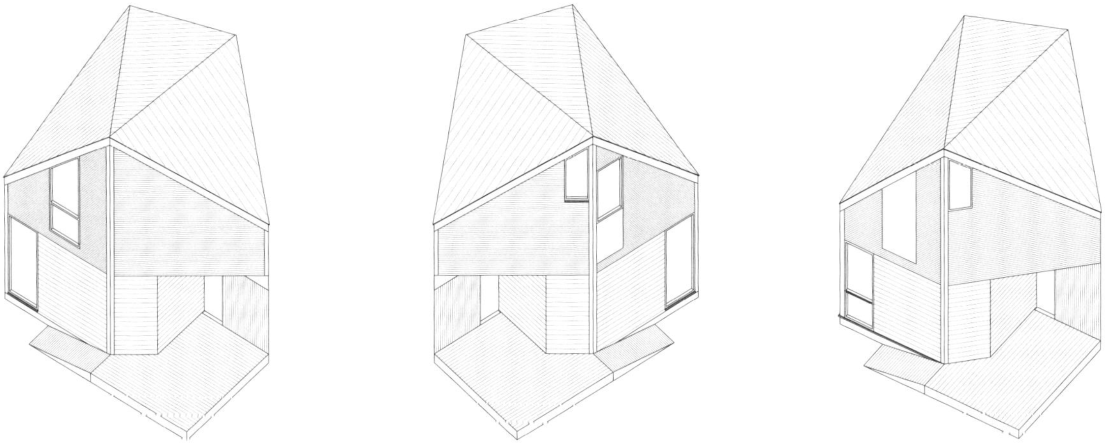

Stan Allen Architect, E/V House & Studio; axonometric studies, 2015

too, approximating the appearance of the building and faithfully describing the internal relationships of the parts. The axonometric is a utilitarian drawing, explaining form and assembly clearly and concisely.

In a 90-degree (or zero-degree) axonometric, the plan is square to the plane of projection. If the power of the axonometric is to combine in one drawing the measurability of orthographic projection with the pictorial character of perspective, the 90-degree axonometric complicates and challenges the descriptive character of the axonometric. It produces an oddly flattened figure on the page, sometimes difficult to read. For me, these projections have a slightly awkward, even naive quality, something almost child-like or coming from somewhere other than the Western canon of visual representation.

This drawing form, which was originated by John Hejduk in the early 1960s, has a strong affiliation with painting. In his diamond projects, Hejduk transposed the painterly problem of the edge of the canvas to the architectural question of the envelope. In the 90-degree axonometric, both plan and front elevation are undistorted, and the sides have collapsed to nothing. The drawing sits frontally, square to the page, forcing a reading of surface and depth, push and pull, onto the architectural object. By the late 1970s, the 90-degree axonometric had become an available technique, no longer necessarily tied to Hejduk's formal language or its associations with Purist painting. Stanley Tigerman, James Stirling, Toyo Ito, and Arata Isozaki all used the 90-degree axonometric to different ends.[1] Hejduk may have originated the form, but it now belongs to the shared culture of the discipline.

I studied with Hejduk at Cooper Union in Manhattan, but as a student I avoided the 90-degree axonometric. With time and distance, Hejduk's work has become more important to me, and I have returned to the 90-degree axonometric. For small-scale projects, this drawing type underlines the building's object-like character while still gesturing to site and context. For me, it is an indirect form of representation, less transparent to the artifact represented. It calls attention to the drawing as artifice.

These new axonometrics are made on the computer, which raises another series of questions. The computer automates operations once done by hand. In most cases, these new axonometrics are not projected from plans; instead, they are oblique orthographic views of a three-dimensional computer model. Strictly speaking, then, although they *look* like them, these quick studies are not true axonometrics. Because the angled edges are foreshortened differently, the dimensional consistency is not preserved. For more developed drawings there is a simple workaround that yields a proper axonometric. It involves a "make 2-D" top view of a 3-D model that has been rotated and sheared at 45 degrees. But it is also worth emphasizing that, for me at least, this yields a fairly crude underlay, which has to be extensively reworked in 2-D, utilizing all of the techniques of projection and geometric construction once done by hand, now faster and more precise in the computer.

Stan Allen Architect, New Maribor Art Gallery, competition, 2010; exploded axonometric from below

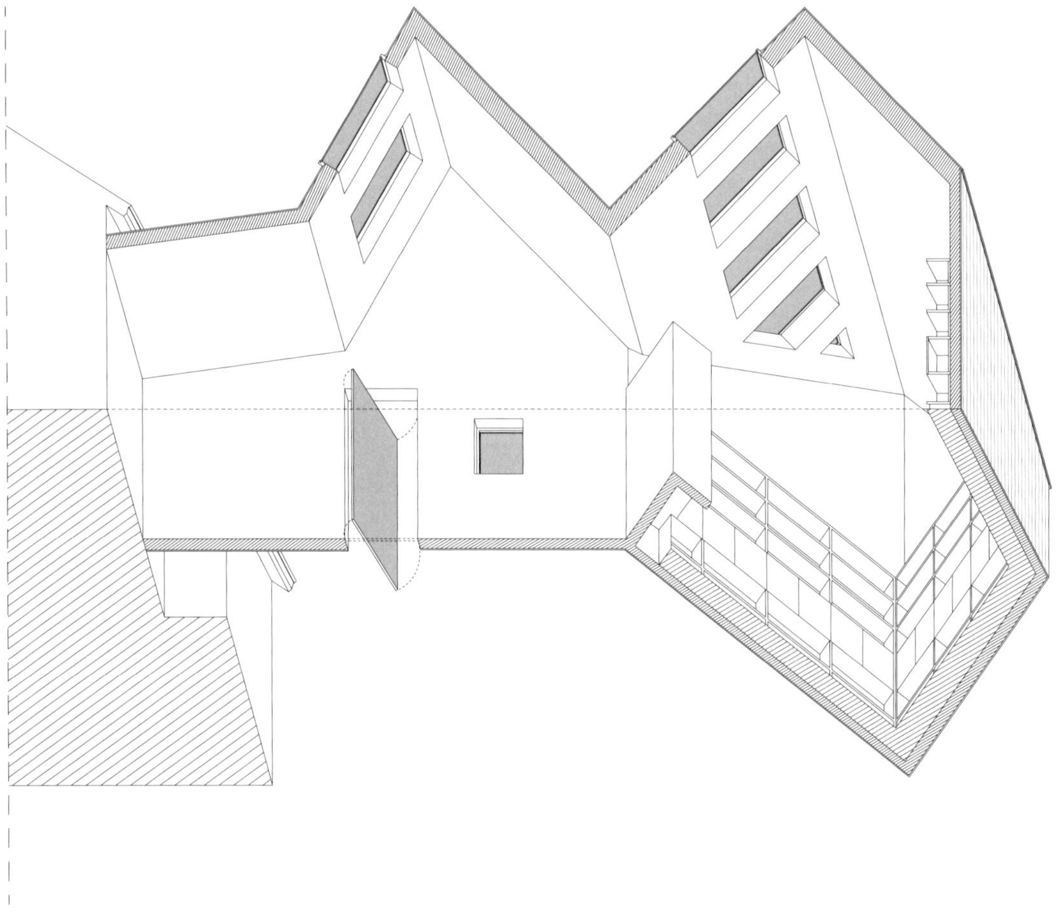

Stan Allen Architect, K/S Library; sectional axonometric

The axonometric is an analytical drawing and lends itself to sectioned, or exploded, views. Originating in military and engineering practice, axonometric drawing was a useful tool to explain the construction and assembly of complex objects and machines. This is true in architecture, too, although it only appeared there later, with Auguste Choisy at the end of the nineteenth century. Choisy cut buildings in plan and section, and adopted the worm's-eye view to explain the pathways of structural forces. The worm's-eye in particular accentuates the relationship between plan and structure. By definition, a worm's-eye must be cut at plan level, and the logic of the structure as it develops upward is clearly explained. These are highly abstract drawings with no reference at all to context or the ground.

What the worm's-eye viewpoint does better than almost any other form of representation is to describe the spatial logic of a three-dimensional enclosure. The 90-degree axonometric is about the building as object; the worm's-eye is about interior space. Plan anticipates movement, structure, and spatial organization, and section maps out profile and scale, but it is fundamentally the domain of the ceiling—domes, vaults, and skylights—that conditions our perception of space. The first thing anyone does upon entering an expansive space is to look up. The worm's-eye allows the architect to study and describe the enclosing effect of the architecture overhead, which is why Choisy employed the worm's-eye view to explain vaulted construction.

The axonometric is, preeminently, an "architect's drawing" technical and precise. It is objective in both senses of the word:

detached, tangible, and impartial, and tending to render the architecture as an object. The drawings made for this book develop out of axonometric studies completed over the course of the design work, but at a certain point, particularly when the buildings are complete, they acquire a logic of their own: as a powerful explanatory tool, and as independent artifacts.

1. A drawing done in 1925 by the Swedish architect Sigurd Lewerentz complicates this chronology. His view of the Resurrection Chapel at the Woodland Cemetery in Stockholm combines plan and elevation to highlight the role of the portico in terminating the long, wooded allée of the cemetery. Although celebrated for his improvisational details, Lewerentz was an extraordinary draftsman, and this is a very sophisticated drawing. Rather than see it as anticipating the 90-degree projections of the later twentieth century, I would see it in the context of naive depictions of towns and settlements common in the nineteenth century. The longitudinal roof of the church, for example, is not projected, and the pavilion overlooking the sunken garden is oriented in the opposite direction. This does not diminish Lewerentz's invention, but rather underscores his originality in adapting a vernacular form, and his commitment to describing the relationship between building and landscape.

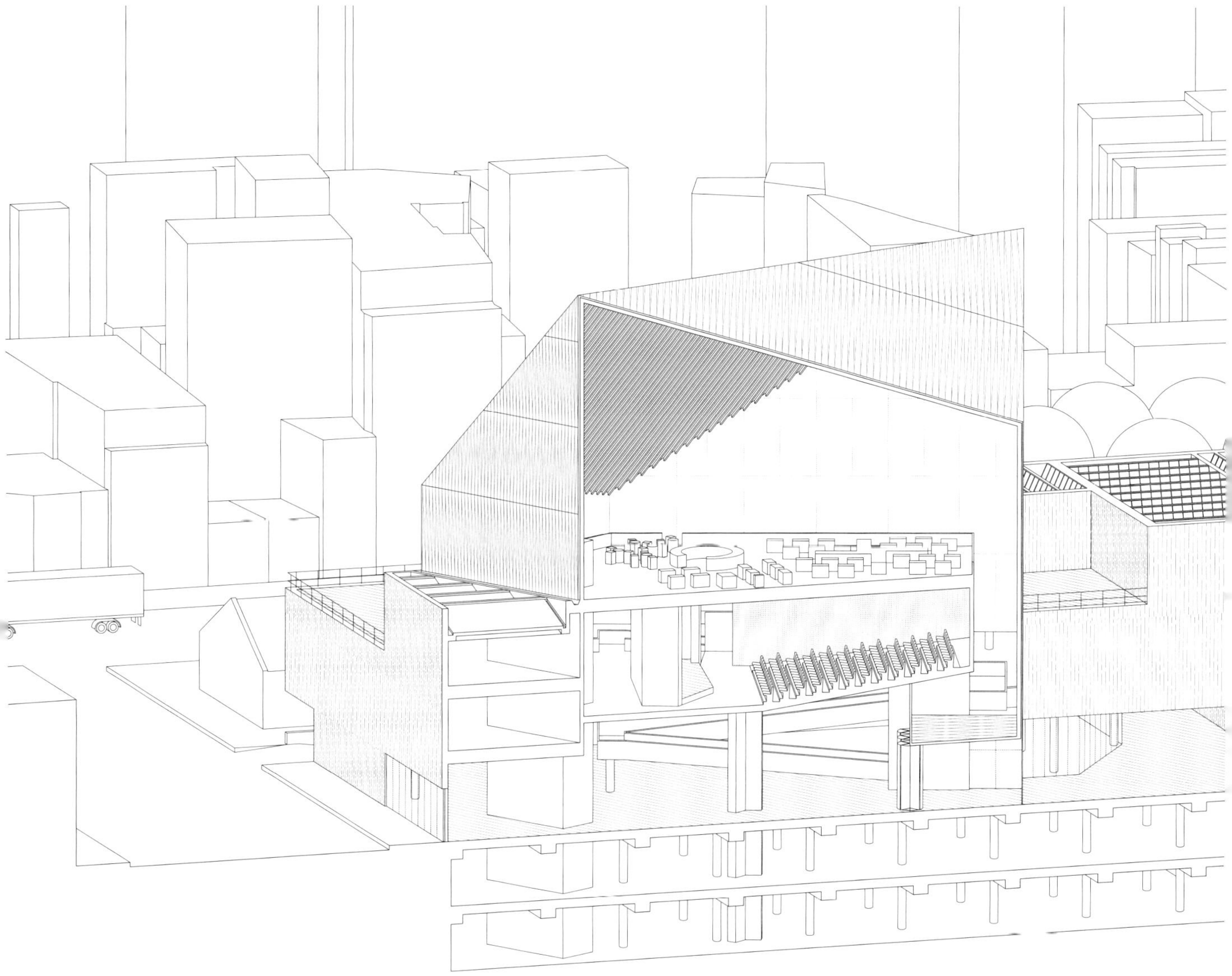

Stan Allen Architect, Tainan Art Museum, Tainan, Taiwan, 2015; cut-away axonometric

Acknowledgments

Architecture is a collaborative art form and many people contributed to the work published here: Liam Turkle, Hans Tursack, Okki Berendschot, Devin Dobrowolski, Steven Sculco, Marc McQuade, Giancarlo Valle, Chris Oliver, Michaela Friedberg, Sean Rucewicz, Michael Toste and Yshai Yudekovitz all worked on the exhibition projects and built work; Liam Turkle in particular has been instrumental in the built projects. That said, my office is small, and most of the drawings in the book are mine – at least in the early stages. The following contributed to the book: Hans Tursack, Liam Turkle, Steven Sculco, Steve Martinez, Naomi Steinhagen, and above all, Andrea Ng. Andrea refined and corrected nearly every drawing in this book, a mammoth task that she completed flawlessly while under quarantine in the complicated months of spring 2020.

Without Scott Benedict's photographs this would have been a very different book. Our collaboration dates back to 2015, and it was his persistence in sending me black & white images of each shot he took that first provoked me to think about a book that could be exclusively black & white photographs and line drawings. Luis Vassallo, the graphic designer, made sure that a monochrome book did not need to be a monotonous book; he brought a keen eye and subtle sense of play to the material. The editor, Lisa Schons at Park Books, shepherded the project through the intricate process of realization. In particular I appreciate her early support. Finally, special thanks to Helen Thomas and Jesús Vassallo for their insightful texts. I should also say that many of the ideas in my texts in this book owe something to an ongoing conversation with Jesús, going back more than ten years now.

The realization of this book would not have been possible without the generous support of the Graham Foundation for Advanced Studies in the Fine Arts, a grant from the Barr Ferree Foundation Fund for Publications, Department of Art and Archaeology, Princeton University, as well as additional support from Princeton's School of Architecture.

Project Credits

M/M HOUSE & STUDIO

Structural Engineer:
Robert Silman Associates

Landscape Architects:
Edwina von Gal/Brian Higley

E/V HOUSE & STUDIO

Structural Engineer:
Michael E. Carr

J/S HOUSE

Structural Engineer:
Proper and O'Leary

Landscape Architect:
Jamie Purinton

L/B STUDIO

Structural Engineer:
Covenant Engineering

Landscape Architect:
Gregg Bleam

Image Credits

PHOTOS OF STAN ALLEN BUILDINGS AND MODELS:
Unless otherwise noted: Scott Benedict,
© scott benedict / practical(ly) studios
Michal Moran: Sagaponac House, p. 11
Michael Biondo: M/M House & Studio, p. 12

EDITORIAL ILLUSTRATIONS:

p. 9	Christian Herron (Delay Tactics)
pp. 18, 103	The Architectural Archives, University of Pennsylvania by the gift of Robert Venturi and Denise Scott Brown.
pp. 99, 100	© The Lane Collection. Photograph Museum of Fine Arts, Boston
p. 101	© Walker Evans Archive, The Metropolitan Museum of Art. Image source: Art Resource, NY
pp. 102, 103	©2020 the Morley Baer Photography Trust, Santa Fe. Used by permission. All rights reserved.
p. 102	Courtesy Haystack Mountain School of Crafts.
p. 103	Courtesy of Turner Brooks Architect; Photograph by Eric Borg
p. 117	Photo by William Henry Jackson; The National Anthropological Archives, Smithsonian Institution.
p. 118, 238	Courtesy of Tigerman/McCurry Architects
p. 185	© The Museum of Modern Art/Licensed by SCALA / Art Resource, NY; © 2020 ProLitteris, Zurich
p. 186	Courtesy of the artist; Lehmann Maupin, New York, Hong Kong; greengrassi, London and the Sterling and Francine Clark Art Institute, Williamstown, MA; Photograph: James Ewing / JBSA
p. 191	Courtesy of Olana State Historic Site; New York State Office of Parks, Recreation and Historic Preservation
p. 238	© ArkDes Collections; Arkm.1973-05-08762

Concept:
Stan Allen

Publication Assistant, SAA:
Andrea T. F. Ng

Copy editing:
Colette Forder

Proofreading:
Lisa Schons

Graphic design:
Luis Vassallo

Pre-press, printing,
and binding:
DZA Druckerei zu
Altenburg GmbH, Thuringia

Paper: 135 g/qm
Symbol Tatami white
Typefaces: Raw, Aperçu
and Untitled Serif

Park Books
Niederdorfstrasse 54
8001 Zurich
Switzerland
www.park-books.com

Park Books is being supported by the Federal Office of Culture with a general subsidy for the years 2016–2020.

ISBN 978-3-03860-204-0

This publication was made possible in part with support from the Graham Foundation for Advanced Studies in the Fine Arts and the Barr Ferree Foundation Fund for Publications, Department of Art and Archaeology, Princeton University.